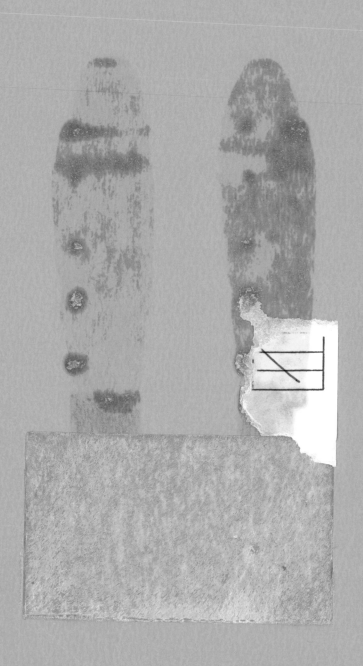

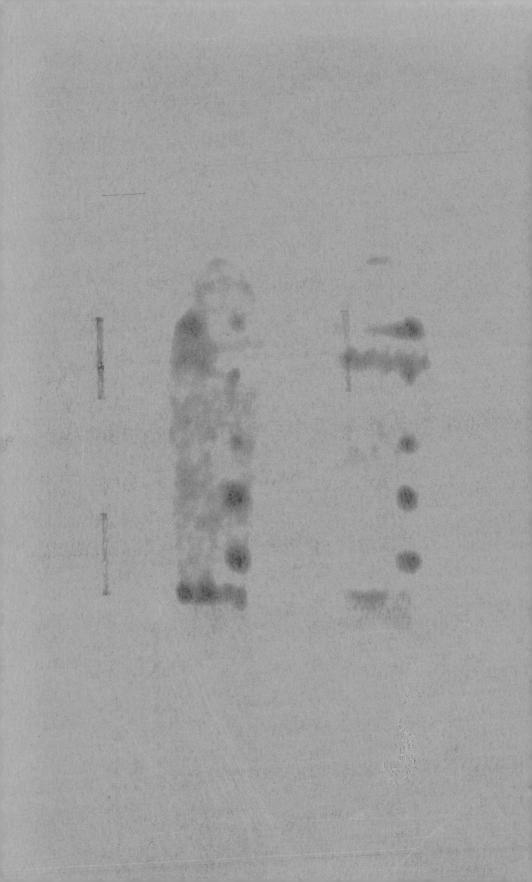

Richard
LESTER

a guide to
references and resources

A
Reference
Publication
in
Film

Ronald Gottesman
Editor

Richard
LESTER

a guide to
references and resources

DIANE ROSENFELDT

G.K.HALL &CO.

70 LINCOLN STREET, BOSTON, MASS.

Library of Congress Cataloging in Publication Data
Rosenfeldt, Diane.
  Richard Lester

  (A Reference publication in film)
  Bibliography: p.
  Includes indexes.
  1. Lester, Richard, 1932-   I. Title.   II. Series.
PN1998.A3L4797   791.43'0233'0924   [B]   78-1277
ISBN 0-8161-8185-3

This publication is printed on permanent/durable acid-free paper
MANUFACTURED IN THE UNITED STATES OF AMERICA

Contents

Preface

Notes on the compilation of this book:

Biographies: The biographical section is a synthesis of information culled from a number of articles and interviews. It was written
chiefly with the help of interviews by film critics Joseph Gelmis,
Ian Cameron, and Mark Shivas. Basic facts were extracted from the
1969 volume of Current Biography.

Synopses and credits: An asterisk (*) preceding an entry number
in this section indicates that I have not seen the film and that my
information is based on secondary sources. In these instances the
synopsis was based on any available published synopses and, whenever
possible, the original work upon which the film was based. When I
was familiar with the film, I wrote from memory, checking myself,
again, against published synopses and original works. Credit lists
were culled from the most complete published lists available. For
synopses and credits, Filmfacts and the British Film Institute's
Monthly Film Bulletin were consistently helpful.

Bibliography: The entries in this section cover a time span from
1960--when Lester started attracting notice--to 1977. The entries are
as comprehensive as possible. I consulted every available film index,
as well as other relevant indexes. I also searched through a volum-
inous amount of unindexed material. Research was done in the Wyllie
Library-Learning Center of the University of Wisconsin--Parkside; the
Gilbert M. Simmons Library (both in Kenosha), and in the Memorial
Library of the University of Wisconsin-Madison; I also used some materials from the University of Southern California.

In this bibliography, the initials [BFI] in Monthly Film Bulletin
entries stand for British Film Institute. The initials [NB] after an
entry indicate that I found the newspaper article in News Bank, a mi-
crofiche system which reproduces articles and reviews from papers
across the country. The articles are arranged by subject and printed
in full except for page numbers and sometimes, unfortunately, by-
lines. In such cases I have listed the entries as "Anonymous." Full
bibliographical information for News Bank is as follows:

News Bank Review of the Arts: Film and Television.

1975: Greenwich, Connecticut, 1975.
1976: Greenwich and Stamford, Connecticut, 1976.

Most underground newspaper entries are from the Underground Newspaper microfilm collection of Bell and Howell and the Underground
Press Syndicate. I found microfilm editions of newspapers and the
several volumes of the New York Times Film Reviews to be very helpful.

Citations with an asterisk denote articles I have not personally
seen. For these I have noted my sources for the citation in brackets
after the entry. In some cases the full bibliographical citations
were too unwieldy to reproduce fully. These appear below.

British Humanities Index 1965. Edited by Peter Farriday. London:
    The Library Association, 1966.

British Humanities Index 1970. Edited by Betty M. King, A.L.A.
    London: The Library Association, 1971.

In the case of foreign-language articles, I have tried to translate
all but the most obvious titles. I have not translated titles in
languages unfamiliar to me. Whenever possible I have based my anno-
tations on my own rough translations; otherwise I have scanned the
article for key words.

Acknowledgments: I would like to thank Ron Gottesman for his interest, guidance and friendship. I am also grateful to my parents,
Dorothy and Ralph, and to countless friends for enduring my monomania
as I prepared this book; to Peggy Runge for divers invaluable aid; to
the Story family, Alberta, Larry, Amy, et al. for food and general
moral support (not necessarily in that order); and to Antoinette
Bloxdorf and Jockey International for unwittingly providing me with
the time and resources to begin my researches.

Early Biographical Background

Richard Lester was born 19 January 1932 to Elliott and Ella Lester, in Philadelphia, Pennsylvania.

A budding genius, Lester entered first grade at the age of three. His parents, not Quakers themselves, enrolled him in a Quaker school, the William Penn Charter School near Germantown, Pennsylvania. Richard completed his high school education when he was fifteen.

Lester's first show-business interest was not films but theatre. (He had seen few films as a child, living several miles from the nearest movie house.) By the time he entered the University of Pennsylvania, he was keenly interested in theatre. He became a member of the Mask and Wig Club and the Pennsylvania Players, for whom he wrote some plays of dubious merit, and composed music for college revues. He was also a member of a vocal ensemble which appeared briefly on a local TV station.

Lester graduated in 1951 with a Bachelor of Science degree in clinical psychology--which he promptly disregarded to go into show business. The singing-group job led to a position at the TV station; he worked his way up to the rank of director in five months. During the two years he stayed there, he received invaluable practical instruction about TV and all facets of production.

Knowing that he was a fast riser, ripe for success, Lester chose to reject it and quit his television station job. He found he had no interest in the routine affluence he was heading for, and opted to abandon the pursuit of it, at least temporarily. Instead, he got three small newspapers to pay him ten dollars a week each as a "roving correspondent" and went to Europe. He tried to supplement this sparse income by playing jazz piano in bars, and by running money across the Straits of Gibraltar to Algiers, where the rate of exchange made Spanish money worth a little more. During this time he became a member of a jazz trio.

Lester arrived in England in 1955 with a musical comedy script to sell. It was bought by a production company and appeared on commercial TV as <u>Curtains for Harry</u>. Lester found that his experience with

1

TV in the States was extremely valuable in England, where commercial television was a new industry. He was given his own short-lived (one performance) show, co-hosted by Alun Owen who would later script <u>A Hard Day's Night</u>. He then became involved in the project which launched his filmmaking career and provided the germ of what is now called the "Lester style"; the television <u>Goon Shows</u>. These shows, starring Peter Sellers, Spike Milligan, and Harry Secombe, were off-shoots of a radio series of the same name. They went under a variety of titles--<u>A Show Called Fred</u>, <u>Idiot's Weekly</u>, <u>Son of Fred</u>. The shows were live, consisting of surreal and non-sequitur skits. Lester, as director, began filming short sight gag inserts to fill air time left by live gags gone wrong. These little films broadened the possibilities open to the show's creators and gave Lester his first experience in filming slapstick.

While working on these shows, Lester began making TV commercials, which not only brought in money but also gave him priceless experience in film techniques and taught him the value of economy in putting across a point. Throughout his career Lester has continued to do commercials to sharpen his skills and to experiment with new techniques and equipment.

On 27 August 1956, Lester married Deidre Vivian Smith, a British ballet dancer and choreographer. Lester did more TV work, including directorial work on thirteen episodes of <u>Mark Sabre</u>, an adventure series about a one-armed detective. Then, in 1957, the Lesters left England, partly because they disapproved of the country's behavior in Suez and partly because they wanted to travel. Their extended round-the-world honeymoon brought them to Canada, where they both worked for the Canadian Broadcasting Company for a time. Then they returned to England and Lester again worked in the television industry. His projects included a pilot for a jazz series, <u>Have Jazz, Will Travel</u>, and another <u>Goon Show</u>. He also composed, along with Reg Owen, the score for the series <u>Sea War</u>, a documentary similar to <u>Victory at Sea</u>.

One day in 1959 Lester had dinner with Peter Sellers, and they began formulating ideas for a short, Goonish film. Somewhere between the soup and the dregs of the wine, <u>The Running, Jumping, and Standing Still Film</u> was born.

Critical Survey of Oeuvre

The name of Richard Lester evokes images of the Beatles, slapstick humor, shock cuts, visual puns, and rapid-fire, almost subliminal, editing. Other Lesterian traits are trendy, blithe cynicism, irreverence, and a comparatively mild and good-natured anti-establishment bias. His films are characterized by disembodied bits of dialog, muttered asides, and plentiful activity on the periphery of the film frame. Generally, one remembers situations rather than characters in Lester films.

All this has been, and basically remains, part of the Lester style. However, the style itself has subtly changed and matured with time, re-emerging within the last few years with increased sophistication, but with no lessening of the comic sense and slightly outré worldview that established Lester as one of the luminaries of the cinema of the sixties.

Lester's beginnings in film were auspicious. As director of the variously-titled television <u>Goon Shows</u>, he often found himself a bit short of material on these live broadcasts. He started filming little bits of nonsense to fill the remaining minutes. A few years later he and Goons Spike Milligan and Peter Sellers shot <u>The Running, Jumping, and Standing Still Film</u> (1959). It is a plotless <u>mélange</u> of sight gags, pratfalls and visual humor in the tradition of the early screen comedies. Like these early films, it has no dialog, although there is a musical score composed by Lester. The finished film incorporates virtually every foot of film shot--a filmmaker's dream in microcosm. Even at this early stage Lester's rather dark comic vision is evident-- at the film's end, the field in which the actors are cavorting opens to engulf them. The film was nominated for an Academy Award.

Lester's first feature film was <u>It's Trad, Dad</u> (known, or rather, unknown in the States as <u>Ring-a-Ding Rhythm</u>) (1962), a rapid-fire potpourri of twenty-six songs in seventy-three minutes, designed to cash in on the current jazz craze in England. Most of the artists and songs are now forgotten, but in 1962 some of them were luminaries of pre-Beatles rock'n'roll: Gene McDaniels, Gary (U.S.) Bonds, and Acker Bilk. The McDaniels footage was shot in New York (Lester paid for his own plane transportation, which indicates extraordinary cheapness and nerve on his studio's part); however, most of the film was shot in a studio which Lester had outfitted with modular sets requiring only a few minutes' rearrangement. He used television techniques; three cameras to film each musical number three times, providing nine different shots from which to choose when editing. Lester was thus able to produce a fairly sophisticated finished film very quickly and inexpensively.

The trifle of a plot that is sandwiched between the musical numbers, concerning a town whose mayor bans rock'n'roll, somehow manages, according to Alexander Walker,[1] to reveal flashes of the Lester satirical wit. However, It's Trad, Dad was largely ignored by critics, who apparently dismissed it as typical of the pop-film genre.

The Mouse on the Moon (1963), the sequel to the highly successful The Mouse that Roared, was a mixed blessing for Lester. His creativity was bound by the restrictions imposed by the previous film; he could only do a workmanlike job. The cast was excellent—actors such as Margaret Rutherford and Ron Moody—but Lester lacked the vitalizing force of Peter Sellers, who had played three roles in the first film. The result was, according to the critics, an undistinguished example of dotty British comedy, intermittently funny but not as inspired as its predecessor. At least it had given Lester an opportunity to practice his craft; it also brought him into contact with its producer, Walter Shenson, whose next project was to be a film about a contemporary social phenomenon—the Beatles.

A Hard Day's Night (1964) was, unlike The Mouse on the Moon, creatively as well as financially rewarding. Spending some preproduction time with the Beatles, Lester was struck by the claustrophobic nature of their lives, and wanted to convey this feeling in his film. He chose a semi-documentary style, a staged cinéma-vérité account of approximately one day in the life of the Beatles. The plot is nearly nonexistent: the Beatles travel to London and do a TV show. However, like a ballet whose skimpy plot (prince meets swan, prince loses swan) is fleshed out with terpsichorean set-pieces, the film is rich with vignettes of varying moods. In them the Beatles are seen together—on a train, in a field, performing, partying—and separately—wandering through the TV studio or "parading."

The cinéma vérité style worked well for the Beatles, displaying their insouciant charm. Although Lester didn't—and still doesn't—leave much leeway in his tightly structured screenplay for ad-libs, and carefully coached the Beatles in the delivery of their lines, he found them capable of witty improvisation. This is evidenced by the press conference scene and the celebrated romp in the field. Both these scenes also illustrate the hemmed-in quality of the Beatles' lives. In the first, the four are jammed into a room full of people, denied the freedom even to grab a sandwich off the sideboard. The other is an expression of their exhilaration at finding freedom of

---

[1]Hollywood U.K. (New York: Stein and Day, 1974), p. 221.

time and space--a moment of time free from commitments, and a space devoid of people who crowd them, bore them, and deprive them of fun.

The movie is full of visual wit: John goes under with his toy boat in the bathtub, then reappears magically elsewhere; a thief breaks into a car, only to have it commandeered by a policeman; Grandfather McCartney rises through the stage floor during the Beatles' performance. However, Alun Owen's screenplay is also sophisticated and witty, with rapid-fire throwaway lines that suit the Beatles' Liverpudlian patois. The camera work is fast and fragmented; although carefully planned it has the look of true cinéma vérité.

The critics reacted to A Hard Day's Night with shock--and pleasure. Haunted by images of the vapid pop extravaganzas of Frankie Avalon, Annette Funicello, and Elvis Presley, most reviewers grimly anticipated more of the same. Instead, they found the film breezy, stylish, satirical and fun--filmed, moreover, in the literate manner of Godard, Truffaut, and the rest of the New Wave directors. The use of Beatles songs on the soundtrack during non-performance scenes, moreover, made the music nearly painless for the critics, and put the film a cut above those pop films which inject badly lip-synched numbers arbitrarily, regardless of logic and taste.

Although A Hard Day's Night is a product of the attitudes and moods of the sixties, it has borne up well over the years, still looking fresh and original--a formidable feat, considering the countless films and TV programs that have borrowed Lester's style and techniques without possessing the satirical intelligence behind them.

Lester seemed to be infallible. His next film, The Knack (And How to Get It) (1965), winner of the Golden Palm at the Cannes Film Festival, was still another look at youth in "Swinging London." Lester and scriptwriter Charles Wood fragmented the Ann Jellicoe play on which it was based, then reassembled it in a purely cinematic way. The play had depended on certain speech rhythms to put across its lightning dialog; Lester and Wood retained this quality and gave it visual equivalents as well. The Knack was filmed in the same freewheeling, pseudo-vérité, New Wave style that A Hard Day's Night had used, employing Lester's habitual three-camera technique--two cameras in blimps (soundproof housings to muffle the sound of the motors) and one hand-held by Lester himself. Many of the numerous London street scenes in The Knack were filmed "on the hoof," since the crew had no police cooperation and were continually being moved along. For these quick takes, two cameras were trained on the action, while a third, hidden one was focused on the frowning faces of passersby. These shots, with appropriate remarks added to the soundtrack, are the Greek chorus of puzzlement and disapproval that runs through the film.

Most critics found The Knack, like the Beatles film, fresh, bright, and innovative. It became obvious that A Hard Day's Night wasn't a fluke, and Lester's reputation began to grow in English-speaking countries and on the Continent.

A second Beatles film was needed. Help! (1965) presented some interesting problems for Lester and his scenarist. The group had already been shown working, and their leisure-time activities were unfit fare for teenaged audiences. Lester and Charles Wood decided that the plot would have to be the "star" and the Beatles would have to be moved by it. The elaborate treatment that resulted had to be scrapped when they discovered that French director Philippe de Broca was filming an identical story. Starting again, Lester and Wood developed the farcical plot of Help! With their expanded budget, color film and location work were welcome novelties for Lester. The resulting film was slicker, but it was generally considered to be somewhat labored in comparison with its anarchic predecessor. Some critics objected to the abundance of action at the expense of character; the Beatles themselves expressed the opinion that they were guest stars in their own movie.

The plot is merely a skeleton on which to hang the countless slapstick jokes, disjointed repartee, and surreal situations. As in the Buster Keaton films Lester reveres, the Beatles are surrounded by zany, inimical mechanical contraptions: the molecule loosening, pants-dropping device and Relativity Credenza of Professor Foot; vending machines which hurl oranges; hand-dryers which disrobe; tanks which pursue. These are manned by equally zany inimical people, played by some outstanding comic actors. Chief among these is Leo McKern as the insidious Clang. Roy Kinnear, making his Lester debut as the bumbling Algernon, has graced most of the later films as well with his hilariously put-upon presence. Victor Spinetti, funny as the fussy director in A Hard Day's Night, is funnier still in Help! as the megalomaniac Professor Foot, whose obsession seems to be his failure to get a government grant for purposes of world domination.

The dialog is characteristically swift, sharp, and satirical: The Scotland Yard man detailed to protect the boys sniffs, by way of greeting, "How long do you think you'll last?" Lennon replies amiably, "And what about the Great Train Robbery then?" When Foot blows a fuse at Buckingham Palace with his Relativity Credenza, a resigned maintenance man at the power station remarks, "She's using her hair dryer again." And at one point Clang, at tea with a group of mild-looking Church of England clergy, mourns that the only way to turn youth back toward religion is to reinstate blood sacrifice.

Help!'s equivalent to A Hard Day's Night's field romp is the Alpine sequence, in which the Beatles ski, sled, and sing in a particularly quickly intercut montage. This segment is also an unobtrusive demonstration of the importance of the film's costume designer. The Beatles' clothing, eye-catching throughout the film, is especially clever here. All the cold-weather wear is basic black, but designer Julie Harris coordinated each suit to its wearer's image or trademark. Thus soulful-eyed Paul wears a turtleneck up over his nose, "aloof" George wears a very Victorian caped coat and topper, etc.

A Funny Thing Happened on the Way to the Forum (1966) was, for Lester, a unique filmmaking experience--one which he has taken pains to avoid repeating.

Melvin Frank, scriptwriter for several Bob Hope pictures, produced the film and had originally planned to direct it. Lester found Frank to be a petty tyrant when, uncomfortable with the story, he tried to make changes and was met with inflexibility. The stage play is more in Frank's style than Lester's, being a bawdy vaudeville "turn," bursting with one-liners. The film is basically the same, although Lester was able to have his way in small but important matters. He was able to choose the supporting cast and to rework several of their roles around their talents. He also influenced the décor of the film, showing the squalor of old Rome rather than a musical-comedy equivalent. He tried to film further changes, but was later denied access to the footage.

The habitually amiable Lester became irritable. He has always been a "total filmmaker" and would like to be the only artist to touch his film from its inception to the finished product. Failing this, he has always collaborated closely with his technical and creative personnel, learning about cameras and their capabilities, helping to edit his films, and picking crews who can intuit his needs, like cinematographer David Watkin and editor John Victor Smith. He employs actors who know what he wants or can take his direction intelligently. He is a dictator, although a benevolent one. His lack of artistic control of Forum resulted in continual feuds with Frank.

Still, the film, which is an uneasy mixture of both their styles, deserves more credit than Lester will give it. He concurs with the critics, who said that the impact of Zero Mostel is lessened by close-ups and cutting, and that the final chase is much too long. However, much of the film works, and Lesterian sight gags abound: slaves line up so that gladiators can practice their mace backswings; the hero, Hero, watches a carrier pigeon plummet after he attaches a wax tablet to its leg; the quest for a sweating horse culminates in a steam bath. The cast is excellent, both in Frank's choices (the great clowns Mostel, Phil Silvers, and Jack Gilford) and Lester's (Michael Crawford, Michael Hordern, Kinnear, and the incomparable Buster Keaton).

Not surprisingly, Lester retained rigid control when he undertook How I Won the War (1967). In this anti-war film, which is also an anti-war-film film, he undermines the standard glory-of-war clichés and ridicules the movies that perpetuate these myths.

One of his methods is to reverse the conventions: Goodbody's troop is no "band of brothers" but a constantly quarrelsome lot; their "vital mission" is to build a cricket pitch; in the heat of battle their contempt for Goodbody remains firm, nor do they prove their mettle--they just die. Goodbody does not love each man as a son, and is so unmindful of their deaths that he calls the replacements by their predecessors' names.

Lester undercuts the emotionalism of war movies by refusing to let the audience involve itself with the characters. He repeatedly reminds one that this is a film: each battle is shown in differently-tinted pseudo-newsreel footage, and the casualties later appear tinted similarly to the battles in which they fell; an extra, discussing the potential war in Viet Nam, says he won't be in it because he doesn't like the director.

One of Lester's most effective, but least appreciated, shock methods involves the main principle of slapstick humor: it is funny only when no one is really hurt. In this film Lester often tries to make the audience ashamed of its own callousness by undercutting a laugh with bloodshed.

As might be expected, the critics generally damned or praised How I Won the War according to their own political orientations. Those who could view it dispassionately seemed to think it was an earnest but uneven effort. Many liberal-oriented writers found it morally right but wrong in its approach, and seemed genuinely distressed that it tried so hard and yet failed. Some--but not many--missed its point, taking it for a botched Carry On-type comedy. After an auspicious U.S. premiere in Los Angeles (attended by most of the royalty of the contemporary pop-rock scene), audiences tended to stay away, alienated by either the then-unpopular pacifist viewpoint or by Lester's Brechtian methods.

Petulia (1968) marked Lester's return to the U.S. after fifteen years' absence. It was an unusual film for him to make, considering his previously anarchic films; it was a quiet, non-comedic film with well-developed characters. The "Lester style" is still evident in the rapid-fire, sometimes subliminal flashes back and forward, but it is subdued, used not for comic effect but for story and character development. The film itself is in the values-questioning, quasi-satirical genre which emerged in the late sixties and included The Graduate, Easy Rider, Carnal Knowledge, Bob & Carol & Ted & Alice, and Little Murders.

Shooting the film was a pleasant experience for Lester. His actors--George C. Scott, Julie Christie, Joseph Cotten, Richard Chamberlain, Shirley Knight--were all true professionals. He was without his usual troupe of character actors, but was able to get many of his supporting players from the acclaimed American Conservatory Theatre of San Francisco. He miraculously avoided the difficulties his do-it-yourself methods might have caused with the strongly unionized U.S. technical crews. The local police cooperated wonderfully with him; the residents of the area in which the crew was filming greeted them cordially and threw them a party when they left.

Critical opinion was likewise rewarding. For the most part, Petulia was considered quite a good study of America's empty, affluent society, as well as of the Petulia character herself. It was also a beautiful travelog of San Francisco--a point not missed by many critics.

The Bed-Sitting Room (1969) was a return to Lester's usual environs and methods. The stylization of the film corresponds to its speculative subject matter of life in post-holocaust London. The landscape and situations are surreal, the people involved virtually automatons, carrying on as if nothing has changed. There are twenty people left in London, each the sole survivor of his type, and each true to type despite the total breakdown of social order. The police exhort people to "keep moving" even though there is no traffic; a BBC man walks around with an empty TV cabinet over his head, reading news. A lone peer still clings to his upper-class values despite the fact that radiation poisoning is mutating him into a lower-class apartment (he feels he should at least be a Stately Home).

In spite of the excellent cast of Lester old-hands--Rita Tushingham, Hordern, Kinnear, Spike Milligan--the film was unsuccessful. It caught the imagination of neither critics nor audiences, and was doomed to oblivion. Its advertising slogan, "We've got a bomb on our hands," became embarrassingly apt. In the past few years, however, the film has gained an audience, primarily among college students, and is on its way to becoming an underground classic.

After the financial failure of The Bed-Sitting Room, there was a creative hiatus in Lester's life. Several projected films were never produced. In some cases he couldn't find a backer--an absurd situation for a director with a firm reputation for coming in on schedule and under budget with well-crafted and usually successful films. His long-cherished Flashman project went the way of other ideas titled Pocock and Pitt, Send Him Victorious, and Eff Off. He turned down an opportunity to direct a version of A Clockwork Orange because he felt himself wrong for the job. He spent considerable time making commercials, principally in Italy.

Suddenly, after three years, Lester returned with a vengeance. He undertook to make a star-studded, epic-length film of Dumas' The Three Musketeers. Where the numerous other film versions of the story had stopped after the boisterous first half of the book (or at any rate had kept the tone light by glossing over the religious war and meaningless deaths of the second half), Lester chose to display the whole rich tapestry of the novel. Later, when distributors' demands for shorter films presented him with the prospect of drastically curtailing the film and reducing the roles of the large cast to ciphers, he chose instead to split the film down the middle. After the renegotiation of the contracts of several surprised actors and the filming of some additional scenes, The Three and The Four Musketeers were born. The initial concept of two films released within a few months of one another was thwarted by the distribution system; the year that ultimately separated them hurt the total work. Lester hoped that the films would eventually be re-released as a double-bill, but as of mid-1977 this has been done only occasionally.

9

The film has a cast for whom the word "stellar" is barely sufficient. More importantly, it departs from the usual epic format in which brilliant actors are wasted in nondescript cameo roles. Lester's casting instincts were surprisingly on-target; he sometimes cast against type but he often used the actors' personalities, "images" and talents to special advantage. Each actor brought something unique to his role, and worked well in ensemble as well. Michael York's d'Artagnan is just the right blend of youthful impetuosity, naivete, clumsiness, agility and valor. Oliver Reed's usual cold menace on screen and his well-publicized drinking habits off make him believable as both the paternal drunk of the first film and the melancholy and dangerous husband of Milady in the second. The remainder of the cast is equally fine in less well-delineated parts. Richard Chamberlain as the near-fop Aramis hints at the cold-bloodedness and hypocrisy the character gains in later books, without making him unappealing. And the admirable Frank Finlay, while lacking the elephantine proportions of the traditional Porthos, conveys the character's flashy bluster and nicely complements the other three. Faye Dunaway and Raquel Welch also interact well. Dunaway is the epitome of beautiful menace as Milady--her scenes with Reed in particular are chilling. The less talented Welch, in the thankless role of Constance, competently slips, trips, fumbles, sweetly apologizes, and executes bits of comic "business," most of which involve her chest. Cast against type as the creaky, cunning Richelieu, Charlton Heston attacks the role with a relish not visible in his endless strong-jawed Biblical portrayals. Christopher Lee, the Dracula of several Hammer films, makes a good, arrogant Rochefort. His film image delightfully sets up the audience for his death at d'Artagnan's hand--in a church, impaled by a sword through the heart.

Rounding out the cast, Roy Kinnear is amusingly put-upon as the valet Planchet; Jean-Pierre Cassel's Louis XIII is the ultimate scatterbrain. Geraldine Chaplin is a beautiful, vulnerable Queen Anne of Austria, and Simon Ward is effortlessly imperious as the lovelorn Duke of Buckingham. Spike Milligan appears briefly but hilariously as Welch's doddering, astounded husband.

Lester's treatment of the characters is at once derisive and admiring. All the heroes are fools; they must be to risk their necks for that King and Queen. On the other hand, the characters who are smart and cynical are nasty. Obviously, Lester is on the side of the fools, and so is the audience. Although outwardly cynical, modern audiences have shown, through their acceptance of such films as Rocky and the incomparable Star Wars, that they are inwardly romantic, harboring secret admiration for the kind of larger-than-life heroes represented by the Musketeers. One of Dumas' tenets, as expressed by Athos in a later book, is that the principle of monarchy must be upheld, although individual monarchs may be villains or clods. In this context the Musketeers are admirable, even though Lester good-naturedly satirizes their blind devotion. In both films, under varying circumstances, Porthos asks, with exaggerated politesse, if it would be presumptuous to ask <u>why</u> he is risking his life. In each case Aramis replies, in essence, that yes, he <u>would</u> be presumptuous; their duty is to be good soldiers and die where they're told to. He concludes, "Is life worth so many questions?"

In many ways <u>The Three Musketeers</u> is a throwback to the exhilarating swashbucklers of the thirties and forties like <u>The Mark of Zorro</u>, <u>The Adventures of Robin Hood</u>--and <u>The Three Musketeers</u> starring Gene Kelly. The main difference between these immortals and the Lester film is that each era's world view is reflected in its films. The values of the World War II era are radically different from those of today; after Watergate, My Lai, etc., we have altered our opinion of what constitutes true patriotism, loyalty, honor, courage. We may honor these abstractions in their pure form, but we are now aware that they do not exist that way. In the <u>Musketeers</u> films, there is an opportunistic streak even in the most idealistic characters--a reflection of the philosophy of the cynical seventies.

Unlike most sequels, <u>The Four Musketeers</u> is not "more of the same." Its tone is darker, more melodramatic. The first film is a "caper," whose objective is to recover the Queen's diamonds and preserve her honor. The second is like a vendetta. The Cardinal is after Buckingham, Milady is after d'Artagnan and Constance, and Athos is after Milady. They are all in deadly earnest, and unexpected deaths result. The lighthearted sword free-for-alls of the first become dusty, exhausting, to-the-death scuffles near the end of the second.

Of course, there are still some excellent pieces of fun, such as the scene in which Finlay and Welch escape on stilts through a yard full of savage dogs. Also memorably funny is the Musketeers' breakfast at La Rochelle, during which they knock grenades back at the enemy, using a long loaf of bread as a mashie. A particularly Lesterian gag results when the spiked grenade sticks in the bread; the Musketeers throw the whole loaf at the attackers, who flee with terrified cries of "Bread! Bread!"

The films have a rich look and sound. Part of the first film's excellence is due to Michel Legrand's excellent score, a varied mix of martial themes and lyrical passages reminiscent of Korngold and Newman--but with tongue firmly in cheek. One piece ends with the sound of someone sitting on a bagpipe; another romantic piece, played during d'Artagnan's clumsy conquest of Constance, is punctuated by little squeals of pain and muttered apologies. The best blend of music and image is the food fight at the inn, during which the Musketeers skewer chickens, pierce wine skins, and ultimately walk off with a banquet secreted about their persons, all to the tune of a sprightly piccolo hornpipe. Unfortunately, the second film's Lalo Schifrin score is quite colorless by comparison.

Other artistic splendors are the beautiful sets, photographed exquisitely by David Watkin. With the exception of Ron Talsky's rather

annoyingly stylized dresses for Raquel Welch, the costumes are extraordinary. Like Julie Harris's costumes for Help!, Yvonne Blake's
costumes for the Musketeers are all black, but reflect each man's personality. Athos's doublet, breeches, and fur-trimmed cloak give the
impression of faded richness, a little worn by use and neglect, like
their wearer. Aramis is dressed with tasteful restraint, with elegant
and usually immaculate lace at collar and cuffs. The exaggerated cut
and overornate trimming of Porthos' suit suggests dandyism without
taste, suitable to the blustery character. D'Artagnan is turned out
well, as he would wish, but simply, befitting his poverty. However,
Blake's shining moment is a royal ball at which everyone dresses in
shades of white, pearly gray, and silver, with fanciful and beautiful
animal-motif headdresses studded with pearls. The scene delights the
eye and boggles the imagination.

Critical response to the first movie was generally favorable, most
writers celebrating the return of Lester. A few thought his slapstick
version betrayed the Dumas classic, despite the fact that the book is
itself full of humor. The second film fared a little worse, being a
sequel in a year full of sequels. However, quite a few commentators
noticed and praised its richer texture and heightened emotion. A few
persisted in raving that it was funnier than The Three, thus displaying a certain insensitivity to its nuances.

The Musketeer films proved that the "entertainment" film was still
popular even amid political cynicism and an era of "heavy" message
films. They also sparked renewed interest in the swashbuckling genre,
paving the way for adventure remakes and parodies of variable quality--
from the poor Michael Sarrazin remake of Scaramouche to the wonderful
The Man Who Would Be King of John Houston. They also triggered a re-
discovery of Dumas' exciting stories, including opulent, non-parodi-
cal television versions of The Man in the Iron Mask and The Count of
Monte Cristo with Richard Chamberlain.

In 1974 Lester took a non-Lester project and, within two weeks,
made it his own. He took over the direction of Juggernaut at the last
minute, rewrote the screenplay a bit, and cast most of the supporting
players in that space of time. The story interested him because it
examines moral attitudes in respect to terrorism. In the film the
concerned steamship company head wants to pay the ransom to save the
people on the ship; the police want to pay the ransom so that they
can find and catch Juggernaut; and the Government, which has controls
on both, wishes not to pay, in order to discourage terrorism.

Lester, who had all his career been making "anti" films--anti-war-
film films, anti-pop-film films, anti-adventure-film films--now turned
out an anti-disaster-film film. The genre was fairly new then, and
the field had been dominated by multi-megabuck Irwin Allen cataclysms.
The Allen disasters are characterized by spectacular special effects,
distinguished actors wasted in interchangeable stereotyped roles, lots
of water (whatever the cataclysm, there is always water), and a pop

singer crooning an insipidly "inspirational" song just before all Hell breaks loose. By contrast, Lester's is a quieter film, alternately building and undercutting tension. The only thing his and Allen's films have in common is the water.

It has been pointed out that in this type of film the technology--in this case the bomb--is the star. However, Lester's good leading players--Omar Sharif, Richard Harris, Shirley Knight, David Hemmings, the remarkable Anthony Hopkins, Kinnear, Hordern, and Ian Holm among them--manage at least to give the contraption a run for its money. The people on the ship are the usual cross-section of humanity, but most of them, through the director's subtle manipulation, escape stereotyping. The technical aspects of the movie, including some exciting aerial photography, are up to Lester's high standards, and the screenplay reflects his wit, particularly in the ironical asides of the cynical Harris and Knight characters.

Critics agreed that the film, taut and stylish, is one of the better examples of a rather wearisome though publicly popular genre. An obtuse minority missed the idea that the suspense in the film is purposely undercut and found themselves bored.

Lester's next film, Royal Flash (1975), the realization of his long-cherished desire to film George MacDonald Fraser's Flashman books, is rather a disappointment (although, admittedly, the Dumas films were a tough act to follow).

Fraser, whose screenplay for the Musketeers movies is polished and occasionally reminiscent of Restoration wit ("Is someone riding a buttercup?" Rochefort sneers at sight of d'Artagnan's incredible yellow plowhorse, "Or is it a cheese with legs?") wrote his own adaptation; his novel is a parody of The Prisoner of Zenda in which the coward Flashy must pose as a German princeling. Somehow the film doesn't quite come together, possibly because Fraser's takeoff on Victorian prose doesn't translate well to film, or perhaps because Flashman is too craven to win the audience's sympathy. As usual, the cast is good: Malcolm McDowell as Flashman; Alan Bates as the mercenary Rudi von Starnberg; Oliver Reed as Otto von Bismarck; Florinda Bolkan as Lola Montes; Britt Ekland as Flashy's frigid princess bride (whose sexual awakening by him is as swift and complete, not to say as violent, as Pussy Galore's by James Bond); brief appearances by Roy Kinnear, whose part is completely lost in the U.S. release print; Michael Hordern; and the late, lamented Alastair Sim.

The script is good and vulgarly funny; in one scene, Rudi, coaching Flashy in the prince's mannerisms, watches in distaste as his pupil deals with an itch, then sneeringly reminds him that royalty does not claw at its buttocks. Flashman's narration is peppered with red-blooded, bawdy Victorian slang--his secret of his success with women is "treating 'em hearty." His credo for survival is "Don't kick a man when he's down; he might get up again."

Some of the more amusing scenes come about when Lester, with visual and verbal puns and inverted cinematic clichés, finds equivalents for Fraser's literary parody. In an early scene, Flashman is saved from peril when Rudi swashbuckles through a door transom. When Flashy notices that the door is ajar, Rudi explains, "I do like to make an entrance"--a viable rationale for Flynn, the Fairbankses and the rest under similar circumstances. Much later Bismarck is seen in a close shot, apparently simulating riding a horse against a phony-looking sky--the shot is a replica of a process-shot one might find in a 1940's studio-bound film. The camera pulls back; Bismarck is tapping his foot impatiently as men carrying a large landscape painting pass behind him. Thus the verbal fun of Fraser is given a visual equivalent by Lester; unfortunately, the really inspired moments are few. This, coupled with the lack of joie de vivre which filled the Musketeers movies, made Royal Flash a disappointing follow-up to them.

Throughout the seventies films, a radical change in the Lester style can be seen. Lester, who repeatedly denies having a style, at least by intent, has ceased the frenetic camera tricks of the sixties, and lets the camera just record what it sees, with ironic detachment. To compensate, he fills the film frame with comic action--in the foreground, in the background, in the center, on the periphery--resulting in humor that is more natural and organic. For Robin and Marian (1976) he modified not only his style but his anarchic world-view as well, to tell a simple, non-ironic, truly romantic love story.

The bittersweet story of the last days together of the aging Robin Hood and Maid Marian is the work of James Goldman, who also wrote the scripts for A Lion in Winter and They Might Be Giants. As in these films, Robin and Marian's chief mood is that of gentle, nostalgic romance. Occasionally there is an unabashedly soaring passage of speech which recalls the great romantic films of the past--Wuthering Heights, Random Harvest, Camille.

The film is extraordinarily beautiful to watch, thanks again to cinematographer David Watkin. One of the most memorable shots shows a sunset behind a burning castle, all in reds and golds, with waves of heat coruscating upward. An uncommon number of long shots emphasize the lush greens of Sherwood. Certain tableaux, with their rich color and deep-focus photography (a long shot of Robin and Marian in their medieval dress, looking dwarfed by the sharply defined, sunlit trees, comes to mind) look like the Pre-Raphaelite paintings of Millais, Hughes, or Holman Hunt.

The cast of Robin and Marian is more than usually charming. The fact that it was Audrey Hepburn's first film in years was an advantage; the nostalgia connected with this blends with that of the story. Sean Connery, who improves immeasurably as an actor with each film, is valiant, saucy, stubborn, gentle and irresistible as Robin. Robert Shaw makes the Sheriff of Nottingham wily, witty and surprisingly likeable. Likewise Nicol Williamson, whose performances sometimes seem brilliant but emotionally cold, portrays Robin's devoted Little John in possibly the most moving characterization of the film. Richard Harris (seen briefly as Richard Lion-Heart), Ian Holm, Kenneth Haigh, Ronnie Barker, and Denholm Elliott provide consistently sound support.

Again, critical opinion was mixed. Many felt the Goldman script to be overblown, but others liked the all-out romanticism. Most of the approving critics admitted that the film is flawed--some ideas don't quite come off--but thought that Lester and Goldman should be praised for this lyrical film nonetheless.

Lester's next film, The Ritz (1976), the film adaptation of Terence McNally's Broadway play about a gay bath-house, is his first out-and-out farce since the painful Forum experience. Like Forum, it is not entirely successful. It is an amusing, sometimes hysterically funny movie, but its tight farce structure precludes the usual Lesterian touches; the direction is always competent, but it lacks Lester's usual individualism. The film could be the work of any good comedy director.

All the principal parts are taken by the same actors who had appeared on Broadway, and they all acquit themselves beautifully. The standout performance is that of Rita Moreno as the hilariously untalented Googie Gomez. Jack Weston, Jerry Stiller, Kaye Ballard, Treat Williams, and F. Murray Abraham are also excellent, but the American setting once more precludes the use of Lester's fine comedic repertory company in all but peripheral roles.

Critics were divided. The subject of homosexuality is treated fairly tastefully in the film; there was surprisingly little comment on that aspect of it. One of the main complaints was that Lester's use of close shots undercuts the action of the farce, which in the play depended on the traffic through the rabbit-warren of doors in the opulent, multi-level set.

Since The Ritz, Lester seems to have gone once again into hibernation; information about his future projects is scarce. He has expressed the desire to film his own adaptation of Cyrano de Bergerac and to work with the gifted writers/performers of Monty Python's Flying Circus (whose collective sense of humor is similar to his own). Both projects offer the possibility of further flights of inspired Lesterian fancy.

Film Synopses and Credits

*1   THE RUNNING, JUMPING   (Great Britain, 1959)
    AND STANDING STILL FILM

Synopsis:

This plotless succession of old-style visual gags presents a succession of Types—explorer, hunter, inventor, etc. They cavort, each in his own way, in a field, in which a chasm eventually opens.

Credits:

Director:	Richard Lester
Producer:	Peter Sellers (Sellers Productions)
Screenplay:	Peter Sellers, Spike Milligan
Photography:	Richard Lester (filmed in silent 16mm; printed in 35mm sepia, sound added)
Music:	Richard Lester
Editors:	Richard Lester, Peter Sellers
Cast:	Peter Sellers, Spike Milligan, Leo McKern, David Lodge, Graham Stark, Bruce Lacey, Mario Fabrizi.
Filmed on location in England in a field.	
Distribution:	Columbia
Running Time:	11 minutes

*2   IT'S TRAD, DAD (RING-A-   (Great Britain, 1962)
    DING RHYTHM)

Synopsis:

No plot information is available, except that the film concerns a horde of jazz and pop musicians who converge on a town whose mayor has banned rock-n-roll music.

Credits:

Director:	Richard Lester
Executive Producer:	Milton Subotsky (Amicus)
Screenplay:	Milton Subotsky
Photography:	Gilbert Taylor
Musical Supervisor:	Norrie Paramor
Incidental Music:	Composed by Ken Thorne
Music/Songs:	Performed by:

Chris Barber and his Band ("It's Trad, Dad"; "Yellow Dog Blues"; "When the Saints Go Marchin' In")
Ottilie Patterson ("Down By the Riverside")
Terry Lightfoot and His New Orleans Jazz Band ("Tavern in the Town"; "My Maryland")
Kenny Ball and His Jazzmen ("Nineteen-nineteen March"; "Beale Street Blues")
Gene Vincent and Sounds Inc. ("Space Ship to Mars")
Brook Brothers ("Double Trouble")
The Temperance Seven ("Dream Away Romance"; "Everybody Loves My Baby")
Bob Wallis and His Storyville Jazz Men ("Aunt Flo"; "Bellissima")
Gary (U.S.) Bonds ("Seven Day Weekend")
Del Shannon ("You Never Talked About Me")
Chubby Checker ("Lose Your Inhibition Twist")
Gene McDaniels ("Another Tear Falls")
Mr. Acker Bilk and His Paramount Jazz Band ("In a Persian Market"; "High Society"; "Frankie and Johnny"; "Ring-a-Ding")
Craig Douglas ("Rainbows"; "Ring-a-Ding")
Helen Shapiro ("Let's Talk About Love"; "Sometime Yesterday"; "Ring-a-Ding")
John Leyton ("Lonely City")

Art Director:	Maurice Carter
Editor:	Bill Lenny
Production Manager:	Al Marcus
Assistant Director:	John B. Merriman
Costumes:	Maude Churchill (Helen Shapiro's dresses made to Butterick printed patterns; Craig Douglas' wardrobe by Cecil Gee)

18

Cast:
Helen Shapiro (Helen), Craig Douglas (Craig), Timothy Bateson (Coffee shop owner), Felix Felton (Mayor), Frank Thornton (TV director), Bruce Lacey (Gardener), Hugh Lloyd (Usher), Arnold Diamond (TV panelist), Ronnie Stevens (TV director), Arthur Mullard (Police chief), Derek Nimmo (Head waiter), Mario Fabrizi (Customer in night club), Derek Guyler (Narrator), David Jacobs, Pete Murray, Alan Freeman.

Filmed at a studio in
England and on location
in New York City.
Distribution: Columbia
Running time: 73 minutes
Released: April 1962 (London)

*3   THE MOUSE ON THE MOON   (Great Britain, 1963)

Synopsis:

   The tiny Duchy of Grand Fenwick is in sore need of indoor plumbing. Its finances are threatened when its sole export, wine, starts exploding. To raise money, the Prime Minister, Count Rupert of Mountjoy, applies to the U.S. for a loan, supposedly to develop a moon rocket. The U.S. and Mountjoy both know that he wants the money for plumbing, but since the U.S. is eager to nominally internationalize the moon race, Grand Fenwick is given a million dollars outright. Mountjoy is ecstatic until Grand Fenwick's resident genius, Dr. Kokintz, discovers that the exploding wine is an unlimited source of energy--i.e., the perfect rocket fuel.
   The Grand Fenwick moon shot is not taken seriously by either the States or Russia, which, not to be outdone by the U.S., has contributed a used rocket. The takeoff of the ship creates an embarrassing situation for both powers, and they separately reach the same decision: in order not to appear to be racing Grand Fenwick, they will say they have launched manned rockets in order to lend assistance should the Fenwickians need it. Of course both countries expect their ships to land first and plant their flag. Due to miscalculations on both their parts, the Fenwickian astronauts, Kokintz and Vincent of Mountjoy (Rupert's son), land first. When the irate U.S. and Russian ships land, they come to grief in the soft soil of the moon's surface. The astronauts are given a lift back to earth by the Fenwickians.
   There is much jubilation in Grand Fenwick, not all of it due to the triumphant return of Vincent and Kokintz. In their

absence, Mountjoy has used the considerable unused chunk of the million dollars to install elaborate bathrooms all over the Duchy.

Credits:

Director:	Richard Lester
Producer:	Walter Shenson (A Walter Shenson Production)
Screenplay:	Michael Pertwee, based on the novel by Leonard Wibberley
Photography:	Wilkie Cooper (Eastmancolor)
Cameraman:	Kevin Pike
Music:	Composed by Ron Grainer
Production Designer:	John Howell
Art Director:	Bill Alexander
Editor:	Bill Lenny
Titles:	Maurice Binder
Production Manager:	R. E. Dearing
Assistant Director:	Ross MacKenzie
Continuity:	Eileen Head
Costumes:	Anthony Mendleson
Cast:	Margaret Rutherford (Grand-Duchess Gloriana), Bernard Cribbins (Vincent), Ron Moody (Prime Minister Rupert of Mountjoy), David Kossoff (Professor Kokintz), Terry-Thomas (Spender), June Ritchie (Cynthia), Roddy McMillan (Benter), John Le Mesurier (British delegate), Michael Trubshawe (British aide), John Phillips (Bracewell), Tom Aldredge (Wendover), Peter Sallis (Russian delegate), Jan Conrad (Russian aide), Hugh Lloyd (Plumber), Mario Fabrizi (Valet, Mario), Archie Duncan (American Air Force General), Richard Marner (Russian Air Force General), John Bluthal (Van Neidel), Clive Dunn (Bandleader), Kevin Scott (American Journalist), Guy Dechy (German scientist), Eric Barker (First member), Allan Cuthbertson (Member), Edward Bishop (First American astronaut), Bill Edwards (Second American astronaut), Laurence Herder (First Russian astronaut), Harvey Hall (Second Russian astronaut), Frankie Howerd (Fenwickian), Gerald Anderson, Robin Bailey (Members-- scene 95).

Filmed in England at Pinewood Studios (using

sets from <u>The Mouse That</u>
<u>Roared</u>).

Distribution: United Artists
Running time: 85 minutes (about 7,650 feet)
Released: 3 May 1963 (London)

4   A HARD DAY'S NIGHT   (Great Britain, 1964)

Synopsis:

The Beatles, pursued by screaming fans, board a train to London. As they meet in their compartment, Paul explains that the old man with him is his grandfather, who is "very clean" but has cost a fortune in breach of promise cases. The four are joined by their managers, Norm and Shake, who take Grandfather for coffee.

A Solid Citizen type takes over their half-empty compartment. John, the satirical one, says "Give us a kiss" as the group goes for coffee. They find that Grandfather has gotten Norm mad at Shake for always being taller than him. The boys pacify them and Norm gives Grandfather some publicity stills on request. When the Beatles try to pick up some girls, Grandfather says the boys are dangerous criminals, and drags them away.

Norm, Shake, and Grandfather leave. When the Beatles rejoin them, Grandfather has disappeared. They find him in another compartment, with a girl; he says he's engaged. For safekeeping, everyone ends up in the baggage car, playing cards and guitars, while girls look on through a wire partition.

There are hordes of girls at the London station. However, by stepping lively they get to their car and thence to their hotel. The boys' hopes of night life disappear as Norm orders them to answer fan mail. Grandfather makes some snide comments about Ringo's nose. Ringo's mail includes an invitation to a gambling den which Grandfather unobtrusively confiscates. Norm and Shake leave, and the Beatles seize their chance to go out. Grandfather waylays a butler and, dressed in his cutaway, goes to the casino.

Norm and Shake find and collect the boys at a discotheque, then discover the stripped-down butler and Grandfather's absence. Thinking that he's probably at an orgy by now, they hurry to find it. When they arrive at the casino, Grandfather has won just enough to pay his considerable bill.

The next day the Beatles go to a press conference which has been provided with champagne and lavish food, but the hungry group can't get near it and must spend the whole conference dodging idiotic questions. After this, they go to the stage which is being set up for their TV performance later that day. They are set upon by a frazzled, insecure director who has been hassled by Grandfather, representing himself as a lighting expert. Norm hustles them to a dressing room. They immediately escape to a field, where they run, jump, and fall down. The owner makes them leave and they mutter, "Sorry if we hurt your field, Mister."

Back in the studio, they wander about. John meets a girl who tells him "You look just like him," but, during the course of their conversation she decides he's nothing at all like "him." George finds himself in an office, and is mistaken as an applicant for the job of sycophant to a teen show hostess. Asked about the sponsor's shirts, he declares them to be "dead grotty," and makes contemptuous remarks about the "posh bird" who hosts the show. The ad man, disturbed, arranges to cancel the girl's contract renewal, as his secretary muses, "Is he an early clue to the new direction?" Meanwhile, Grandfather finds himself rising gently through the stage floor in the midst of an opera rehearsal.

The boys return and rehearse. Grandfather is testy, saying that so far he's been in "a train and a room, and a car and a room, and a room and a room," and he's sick of it. He goes off with Ringo, exhorting him to "parade" and encouraging him to feel put-upon by the others. Half an hour before the final run-through, Ringo leaves, and the others go in search of him.

Ringo buys an old coat and hat and wanders about, meeting on his way a boy who discusses his pals. After inadvertently getting into several little scrapes, he is finally taken to a police station. There he finds Grandfather, who has been taken in for selling the publicity pictures and resisting arrest. Indicating the mild-mannered policemen, Grandfather hisses to Ringo, "If they get you on the floor, watch out for your brisket."

Grandfather escapes and tells the others where to find Ringo. They break him out and return to the studio, where they give Grandfather a tongue-lashing. They have missed the run-through, but are in time for the performance, much to the relief of the director, who has been hysterical to the point of absolute calm.

The boys perform. The crowd is noisily enthralled. Even the director begins to relax. Norm and Grandfather are in the audience, handcuffed together. Somehow, Grandfather slips the cuffs; once again he appears through the floor of the stage and is hustled off. The performance ends. The director prepares to have a minor breakdown.

Norm has arranged a getaway by helicopter. Grandfather is already handcuffed to it, clutching his publicity stills. The boys climb on and it rises. Grandfather loses his hold on the photos and they scatter in the air.

Songs: "A Hard Day's Night," "Tell Me Why," "I Should Have Known Better," "I'm Happy Just to Dance With You," "And I Love Her," "If I Fell," "Can't Buy Me Love," "I Wanna Be Your Man," "Don't Bother Me," "All My Loving," "She Loves You."

Credits:

Director:	Richard Lester
Producer	Walter Shenson (Proscenium Films)
Associate Producer:	Denis O'Dell
Screenplay:	Alun Owen
Photography:	Gilbert Taylor
Sound Recorders:	H. L. Bird and Stephen Dalby
Musical Director:	George Martin
Songs:	John Lennon, Paul McCartney
Art Director:	Ray Simm
Editor:	John Jympson
Titles:	Robert Freeman
Assistant Director:	John D. Merriman
Costumes:	Julie Harris
Cast:	John Lennon (John), Paul McCartney (Paul), George Harrison (George), Ringo Starr (Ringo), Wilfrid Brambell (Grandfather, "Mixing" John McCartney), Norman Rossington (Norm), Victor Spinetti (TV director), John Junkin (Shake), Anna Quayle (Millie), Deryck Guyler (Police Sergeant), Michael Trubshawe (Club manager), Kenneth Haigh (Shirt advertising man), Richard Vernon (Pompous traveller), Eddie Malin (Waiter), Robin Ray (TV stage manager), Lionel Blair (TV choreographer), Alison Seebohm (Secretary), Marianne Stone (Gossip), David Langton (Actor), Claire Kelly (Barmaid), Roger Avon, John Bluthal, Pattie Boyd, Margaret Nolan, Terry Hooper, Derek Nimmo, Bridget Armstrong.

Filmed on location in
and around London.

Distribution:	United Artists
Running time:	85 minutes (7,650 feet)
Released:	6 July 1964 (London)

*5   THE KNACK--AND HOW TO   (Great Britain, 1965)
GET IT

Synopsis:

   Timid Colin is desperately in need of female companionship,
but has little success in finding it. He seeks the advice of
his cocky friend Tolen, who is absurdly notorious as a ladies'
man. Their friend Tom, who has just moved in downstairs,

isn't worried about women, being more concerned with painting everything in his apartment stark white. Colin worries that his bed is the cause of his failure. Tom takes Tolen and Colin across the city to a junkyard where resides a huge and preposterous bedstead. En route they encounter Nancy, an innocent from the provinces who, just arrived in London, is looking for the YWCA. She falls in with them and never does find the "Y." The bed is so large that the four of them must float it across the Thames and push it through the streets to get it home. They provoke a constant chorus of disapproval from the Solid Citizens along the way.

Tolen decides to give Colin a practical lesson in seduction, and sets his cap for Nancy. When he feels she's sufficiently in the mood, he lets Colin take over. Colin's inexperience shows and the angry Nancy goes off with Tolen. Tom and Colin follow them. Tolen chases her all through a park until, over-excited, she faints. When she wakes up she claims to have been raped. Tolen is insulted; the accusation is an affront to his slick modus operandi. Colin, convinced that he is responsible for her condition, is pleased--gaining confidence, he undergoes a change in self-image. Tolen tries to reclaim Nancy, but she dismisses him; he has lost the knack. She decides to go with Colin, who has gotten it.

Credits:

Director:	Richard Lester
Producer:	Oscar Lewenstein (Woodfall Productions)
Associate Producers:	Leigh Aman, Michael Deeley
Screenplay:	Charles Wood, based on the play by Ann Jellicoe
Photography:	David Watkin
Cameramen:	Alan Hall, Jack Dooley
Sound:	Richard Bird, Stephen Dalby
Music:	Composed and directed by John Barry; solo jazz organ by Alan Haven
Art Director:	Assheton Gorton
Set Decorator:	James Brennan
Editor:	Anthony Gibbs
Titles:	Robert Freeman
Production Manager:	Jane Moscrop
Assistant Director:	Roy Millichip
Makeup:	Freddie Williamson
Hairstyles:	Betty Sherriff
Costumes:	Jocelyn Rickards
Cast:	Rita Tushingham (Nancy), Ray Brooks (Tolen), Michael Crawford (Colin), Donal Donnelly (Tom), John Bluthal (Angry father), Wensley Pithey (Teacher), William Dexter (Dress

shop owner), Peter Copley (Picture owner), Dandy Nichols (Tom's landlady), Charles Dyer (Man in photo booth), Helen Lennox (Blonde in photo booth), Edgar Wreford (Man in telephone booth), George Chisholm (Left luggage porter), Frank Sieman (Surveyor), Bruce Lacey (Surveyor's assistant), Timothy Bateson (Junkyard owner), Margot Thomas (Woman teacher), Wanda Ventham (Gym mistress), Gerald Toomey (Boy in classroom), Katherine Page (Woman in house), Rose Hiller (Unsuitable customer), Charles Wood (Soldier), Walter Horsbrugh (Old man), Julian Holloway, Vincent Harding, Kenneth Farrington, John Porter Davison (Guardsmen), Charlotte Rampling, Lucy Bartlett (Water-skiers), Dorothy Sue, Lucille Soong, Yu Ling, June Lim (Chinese girls), Vicki Udall, Coralie Persee, Jacqueline Bisset, Anna Biro, Lynn Broadbent, Carol Chilvers, Louisa Cornwall, Sonya Dean, Pauline Dukes, Eve Eden, Liza Firbank, Maren Greve, Susie Holt, Judy Jones, Samantha Just, "Karina," Hanja Kochansky, Annabella Macartney, Judith McGilligan, Jean Nesbitt, Suzanne Owens, Micky de Rauch, Judy Robinson, Geraldine Sinclair, Annabelle Sylvester, Nina Talbot-Rice, Janny White, Susan Whitman (Tolen's girlfriends).

Filmed on location in and around London.

Distribution:	United Artists
Running time:	84 minutes (7,651 feet)
Released:	2 June 1965 (London) (The film had won the Palme d'Or at the Cannes Film Festival a few weeks previously.)

6 HELP!   (Great Britain, 1965)

Synopsis:

Somewhere in the Mysterious East, a young, red-painted girl is about to be sacrificed to the goddess Kaili. At the last moment the priestess Ahme, who is also the victim's sister,

stops Clang, the high priest. The girl is not wearing the
sacrificial Ring; she has sent it as a gift to Ringo Starr.
The Easterners depart for London where they make several attempts to recover the Ring by various James Bondian techniques
in various places: in a vending machine, in a mailbox, in an
elevator, in a men's room and in a recording studio where they
cut a circle in the floor under Ringo's drum set. The Ring,
however, is firmly stuck on Ringo's finger. After a narrow
escape at a restaurant thanks to the warning of Ahme, who has
established a winking relationship with Paul, the Beatles go
to a jeweler, who fails to cut the Ring off. They then go to
the erratic scientist, Professor Tiberius Foot, and his assistant Algernon, who attach Ringo to a machine designed to
enlarge the molecules of the Ring and cause it to drop off.
Instead, his trousers fall down. Foot, recognizing the Ring's
power, determines to get it, and attacks Ringo. The Beatles
are saved by Ahme and flee, leaving Foot to mutter about the
Brain Drain and the lack of government funding in his field.

Back at the boys' communal pad Ahme warns them of Ringo's
great danger; by custom, so far only her sister could be sacrificed, but now her time has expired and it's open season on
anyone wearing the Ring. Ahme has brought a syringe of something which will shrink Ringo's finger, but before she can use
it, it gets stuck in Paul, who suddenly finds himself on the
floor, two inches tall and nude. Clang and his Thugs launch
an attack on the house, as do Foot and Algernon. Paul is
nearly trampled as the Thugs try to drench Ringo with red sacrificial paint. The evil ones are defeated, but a spot of
red paint on someone's shoe makes the Beatles suspect that
they have stepped on Paul, until he just as suddenly returns
to normal size.

The boys try an escape to the Alps but are unsafe there.
After attempts on the Ring at Scotland Yard, Salisbury Plain,
Buckingham Palace, and in the street, they duck into a pub,
where Ringo becomes trapped in the cellar with a tiger. Ahme
pops in to advise him that the tiger can be subdued by singing
Beethoven's "Ode to Joy" from the famous Ninth Symphony. After
a rousing chorus from people up and down the street, Ringo is
saved.

The Beatles go to the Bahamas escorted by the timorous Inspector Gluck of the Yard and followed by Clang, his Thugs,
Foot, and Algernon. More attempts ensue and finally the four,
tired of running, decide to fight it out at the temple of
Kaili, which has been transported there especially for the oc-
casion. They are lured to a deserted spot by the Thugs, only
to have Ringo snatched away by Foot and rescued in turn by
George. Inspector Gluck starts rounding up Thugs using Ringo-
masked Beatles as decoys. Foot spirits the real Ringo off to
his yacht and prepares to operate on him. Ahme sabotages his
equipment and produces a new batch of shrinking fluid. Seeing
the syringe, Foot loses interest in the Ring, sensing even

greater power in the liquid, which he plans to call Sir Tiberius Foot Juice. Escaping, Ahme and Ringo fall back into Clang's hands. Ringo is reddened but at the last moment displays Courage, the one force which will loosen the Ring, and thrusts it on Clang's finger. A melee results. Ahme exhorts the Thugs to deal with the beRinged and red-daubed Clang, but it seems that he has availed himself of Foot Juice. The Ring is passed around and finally foisted on Clang's hapless, battered aide-de-camp Bhuta, who is pursued down the beach by the blood-thirsty mob.

Songs: "Help!," "The Night Before," "You've Got to Hide Your Love Away," "I Need You," "Another Girl," "Ticket to Ride," "You're Gonna Lose That Girl."

Credits:

Director:	Richard Lester
Producer:	Walter Shenson (Walter Shenson/ Subafilms)
Screenplay:	Charles Wood, based on a story by Marc Behm
Photography:	David Watkin (Eastmancolor)
Color Consultant/ Titles:	Robert Freeman
Sound:	H. L. Bird, Stephen Dalby, Bill Blunden, Don Challis
Music/Songs:	John Lennon, Paul McCartney "I Need You" by George Harrison Wagner's Overture to Act III of Lohengrin Beethoven's "Ode to Joy" from his Ninth Symphony
Musical Director:	Ken Thorne
Music Editor:	Barry Vince
Art Director:	Ray Simm
Editor:	John Victor Smith
Production Manager:	John Pellatt
Assistant Director:	Clive Reed
Costumes:	Julie Harris
Cast:	John Lennon (John), Paul McCartney (Paul), George Harrison (George), Ringo Starr (Ringo), Leo McKern (Clang), Eleanor Bron (Ahme), Victor Spinetti (Professor Tiberius Foot), Roy Kinnear (Algernon), Patrick Cargill (Superintendent), John Bluthal (Bhuta), Alfie Bass (Doorman at restaurant), Warren Mitchell (Abdul), Peter Copley (Jeweler), Bruce Lacey (Lawn mower).

27

Filmed on location at
London, Salisbury Plain,
the Alps, and the Bahamas.

Distribution:	United Artists
Running time:	92 minutes (8,280 feet)
Released:	27 July 1965 (London: Royal World Premiere)

7 A FUNNY THING HAPPENED   (Great Britain, 1966)
   ON THE WAY TO THE FORUM

Synopsis:

   The plot of this farce concerns the efforts of a con-man
slave, Pseudolus, to gain his freedom and the woman of his
choice, a Junoesque mute courtesan named Gymnasia (and, inci-
dentally, to escape the killing caresses of the powerfully
built breeder slave who has taken a fancy to him); of his young
master Hero to gain the hand of Philia, a virgin courtesan
living in the bordello next door, who is promised to the war-
rior Miles Gloriosus; of Lycus the procurer to deliver Miles'
goods intact; of Hero's father Senex to philander while trying
to evade the eagle eye of his harridan wife Domina; of Erronius, another neighbor, to find his children, who were lost in
infancy; and of Hysterium, major domo in the house of Senex,
to keep himself safe from the forces of Chaos released by
everyone else's efforts.
   The action involves a love potion made of laboriously
gathered mare's sweat, which keeps coming to grief; rumors of
a plague in Philia's homeland; a ring depicting a gaggle of
geese; a wild chariot chase; a game of musical houses; an orgy;
a phony funeral; several mistaken identities; and a good deal
of cross-dressing.
   All these combine toward the desired result. Senex's marriage is pepped up by the potion (although not in the way he
had hoped for); Erronius discovers that his children are Philia
and Miles. Hero claims Philia, and Miles is given twin courte-
sans who get in return (he says) "the best." Pseudolus gets
his freedom and cons Lycus into giving him Gymnasia for services rendered; he also gets rid of the breeder slave, who has
taken what may turn out to be a fatal fancy to Hysterium.

Songs: "Comedy Tonight," "Lovely," "Everybody Ought to Have a
   Maid," "Bring Me My Bride," "Lovely (reprise)," Funeral Sequence and Dance, "Comedy Tonight (reprise)."

Credits:

Director:	Richard Lester
Producer:	Melvin Frank (Quadrangle)

Screenplay:	Melvin Frank and Michael Pertwee, based on the musical comedy by Burt Shevelove and Larry Gelbart (itself based on the play Pseudolus by Plautus)
Photography:	Nicholas Roeg (DeLuxe color)
Second Unit Photographer:	Paul Wilson
Cameraman:	Alex Thomson
Special Effects:	Cliff Richardson
Sound:	Gerry Humphreys, Lee Hammond
Music/Lyrics:	Stephen Sondheim
Musical Director:	Irwin Kostal
Production Designer:	Tony Walton
Art Director:	Syd Cain
Editor:	John Victor Smith
Titles:	Richard Williams
Choreographers:	Ethel and George Martin
Production Manager:	Clifford Parkes
Assistant Director:	Jose Lopez Rodero
Second Unit Director:	Bob Simmons
Continuity:	Rita Davison
Costumes:	Tony Walton
Associate Costume Designer:	Dinah Greet
Wardrobe Master:	Ray Beck
Cast:	Zero Mostel (Pseudolus), Phil Silvers (Lycus), Jack Gilford (Hysterium), Buster Keaton (Erronius), Michael Crawford (Hero), Annette Andre (Philia), Patricia Jessel (Domina), Michael Hordern (Senex), Leon Greene (Miles), Inga Nielsen (Gymnasia), Myrna White (Vibrata), Lucienne Bridou (Panacea), Helen Funai (Tintinabula), Jennifer and Susan Baker (Geminae), Janet Webb (Fertilla), Pamela Brown (Priestess), Beatrix Lehmann (Domina's mother), Alfie Bass (Gatekeeper), Roy Kinnear (Instructor), Frank Elliott, Bill Kerr, Jack May, Frank Thornton, John Bluthal, Ronald Brody, Jon Pertwee.
Filmed on location in Spain.	
Distribution:	United Artists
Running time:	98 minutes (8,820 feet)
Released:	16 October 1966 (New York City)

*8   HOW I WON THE WAR   (Great Britain, 1967)

Synopsis:

Ernest Goodbody, a soldier of little education and less
breeding, has climbed through the ranks of the military largely
aided by officers who kick him upstairs to get him out of the
way. Thus he becomes a Lieutenant, and is put in charge of
the Third Troop of the Fourth Musketeers, the sorriest bunch
of soldiers World War II is likely to produce. It includes
the buffoon Juniper, the socialist Gripweed, the fearful
cuckold Clapper, the cowardly Melancholy Musketeer, and the
cynical Sergeant Transom.
In North Africa, Goodbody's little band is given a vital
mission. A military V.I.P. is scheduled to pass through soon.
They are to penetrate enemy lines and set up a deluxe cricket
pitch for his benefit. Hopefully the land they will infiltrate
will be taken by the Allies by the time the big man arrives.
Goodbody is separated from his men in the desert but is re-
united with them. Their lack of enthusiasm at his return would
lead anybody but Goodbody to suspect that they had had some
part in the separation. Together they surmount many obstacles:
they must recapture their pitch-roller, which has been stolen
by the Italians. Then they fail to accomplish a mission to
destroy an important German petrol dump. Each sortie costs
lives, but the cricket pitch is completed. The V.I.P. drives
unheedingly past it.
The troop ends up in Germany, trying to capture a bridge on
the Rhine. The numerous fatalities in Goodbody's company have
been replaced, although Goodbody persists in calling the new
men by their predecessors' names. Once again separated from
his men, Goodbody is captured by Commandant Odlebog, the sole
German defender of the bridge. They begin to talk and become
friends. Goodbody finally buys the bridge from the pacifistic
Odlebog, only to see his new friend killed by Allied tanks.
Twenty years later, the still-deluded Goodbody holds a re-
union for his old command. Not surprisingly, the only parti-
cipator, and possibly the only survivor, is the craven Melancholy Musketeer.

Credits:

Director:	Richard Lester
Producer	Richard Lester (Petersham Films)
Associate Producer:	Denis O'Dell
Screenplay:	Charles Wood, based on the novel by Patrick Ryan
Photography:	David Watkin (Eastmancolor)
Special Effects:	Eddie Fowlie
Sound:	Les Hammond, Gerry Humphreys, Don Challis, Alan Pattillo

Music:	Composed and conducted by Ken Thorne
Art Directors:	Philip Harrison, John Stoll
Editor:	John Victor Smith
Production Managers:	Hubert Froelich, Roberto Roberts
Assistant Director:	Pepe Lopez Rodero
Continuity:	Phyllis Crocker
Costumes:	Dinah Greet
Cast:	Michael Crawford (Lieutenant Ernest Goodbody), John Lennon (Gripweed), Roy Kinnear (Clapper), Lee Montague (Troop Sergeant Transom), Jack Mac-Gowran (Juniper), Michael Hordern (Lieutenant-Colonel Grapple), Jack Hedley (Melancholy Musketeer), Karl Michael Vogler (Commandant Odlebog), Ronald Lacey (Spool), James Cossins (Drogue), Ewan Hooper (Dooley), Alexander Knox (American General), Robert Hardy (British General), Sheila Hancock (Mrs. Clapper's friend), Charles Dyer (Flappy-trousered man), Bill Dysart (Para-trooper), Paul Daneman (Skipper), Peter Graves (Staff officer), Jack May (Toby), Richard Pearson (Old man at Alamein), Pauline Taylor (Woman in desert), John Ronane (Operator), Norman Chappell (Soldier at Alamein), Bryan Pringle (Reporter), Fanny Carby (Mrs. Clapper), Dandy Nichols (First old lady), Gretchen Franklin (Second old lady), John Junkin (Large child), John Trenaman (Driver), Mick Dillon (First replacement), Kenneth Colley (Second replacement).
Filmed on location in Germany.	
Distribution:	United Artists
Running time:	110 minutes (9,941 feet)
Released:	18 October 1967 (London)

9 PETULIA   (Great Britain, 1968)

Synopsis:

Petulia Danner, dancing with her husband of six months, David, at a weird charity function, sees Archie Bollen, a divorced doctor. She is attracted to him, and with a sort of desperate, determined kookiness, initiates an affair with him. They visit a motel, after which she returns to the party. The next morning she turns up at his place with a purportedly stolen tuba and a broken rib she says she got falling on the tuba. Archie has another doctor examine her and promises to return the tuba to its owner. He takes it to the address she has given him, but there is no answer to his knock, so he takes it back home with him.

Life continues for Archie. His ex-wife, Polo, a rather vulnerable woman who is still a little bewildered by the breakup of her marriage, visits him to explain that she will need his alimony money until her new boyfriend, Warren, acquires his masters' degree in hydraulics. Archie finds her alternately clinging and desirable. A short time later, Petulia interrupts Archie's outing with his mistress, May, ostensibly to pick up the tuba so she can return it. Archie tries to tell her he has no wish to see her again. However, he does see her, and ultimately sleeps with her, leaving her in bed at his apartment as he goes off to spend a few hours with his kids. He returns to find her beaten almost to death. David, an immature, weak man and a burgeoning sadist, has Found Out.

At the hospital Petulia is visited by David's pompous and overbearing father, who is full of plans for the Danner families, junior and senior, to travel to South America on the family sloop. He bullies the hospital authorities into letting Petulia go home. Archie, coming in and discovering this, rushes to her house, only to be met by a united front of Mr. Danner, David, and Petulia, all of whom insist, in spite of Archie's bald accusations, that her injuries are the result of a dizzy spell and a fall. As Archie leaves in a rage, Petulia remarks to David that she'd have turned Archie's hands into fists. David doesn't quite comprehend her meaning; she tells him that when she first knew <u>him</u>, he had been the gentlest man she'd ever met.

Archie encounters Petulia once more, briefly and by chance; a short time later he arrives home to find that she has ordered a greenhouse installed in his bedroom. With a bouquet from it he goes to her house, but she is with the Danners on the proposed cruise.

On the boat, relations between Petulia and David seem to have improved, but she is very upset when the elder Danners unexpectedly fly home, leaving the two of them alone. They have a long discussion in which he realizes and comes to grips with, at least in part, the reasons for his violence toward her in the past; he promises never to touch her again unless she wishes it. She realizes his need for her, and they become closer to one another.

About a year later Archie and Petulia meet again. She is at his hospital, waiting to give birth to David's baby. Archie asks her to go away with him, and after some hesitation she agrees. He finds himself unable to take the necessary action. They say their farewells and Archie leaves. As Petulia goes into the delivery room, her thoughts are all of him.

Credits:

Director:	Richard Lester
Producer:	Raymond Wagner (Petersham Films)
Associate Producer:	Denis O'Dell
Executive Associate Producer:	Don Devlin
Screenplay:	Lawrence B. Marcus; adapted by Barbara Turner from the novel <u>Me and the Arch-Kook Petulia</u> by John Haase
Photography:	Nicholas Roeg (Technicolor)
Sound:	Francis E. Stahl
Music:	Composed and conducted by John Barry
Production Designer:	Tony Walton
Associate Art Director:	Dean Tavoularis
Design Consultant:	David Hicks
Set Decorator:	Audrey Blaisdel
Editor:	Antony Gibbs
Light Show:	Paul Hawkins
Production Manager:	Emmett Emerson
Location Manager:	Harry Zubrinsky
Assistant Director:	John Bloss
Casting:	Fred Roos
Makeup:	Gus Norin
Hairstyles:	Vivian Zavitz
Costumes:	Tony Walton
Cast:	Julie Christie (Petulia Danner), George C. Scott (Archie Bollen), Richard Chamberlain (David Danner), Arthur Hill (Barney), Shirley Knight (Polo), Pippa Scott (May), Joseph Cotten (Mr. Danner), Kathleen Widdoes (Wilma), Roger Bowen (Warren), Richard Dysart (Motel receptionist), Ruth Kobart, Ellen Geer (Nuns), Lou Gilbert (Mr. Howard), Nat Esformes (Mr. Mendoza), Maria Val (Mrs. Mendoza), Vincent Arias (Oliver), Eric Weiss (Michael), Kevin Cooper (Stevie), Austin Pendleton, Barbara Colby, Rene Auberjonois, Josephine Nichols, De Ann Mears, The Grateful Dead, Big Brother and the Holding Company, Members of The Committee, Members of the American Conservatory Theatre.
Filmed on location in San Francisco and Tijuana.	
Distribution:	Warner/Seven Arts
Running time:	105 minutes (9,422 feet)
Released:	10 June 1968 (New York City)

*10   THE BED-SITTING ROOM   (Great Britain, 1969)

Synopsis:

    The time is three years after the last global "atomic mis-
understanding," which has lasted a bit over two minutes, including the signing and blotting of the peace treaty.
Civilization is, for all practical purposes, dead, and there
are only about twenty people left in London. Penelope, a
young girl who lives with her parents in a tram car, is seventeen months pregnant (presumably by her lover Alan, who lives
in the next car). Penelope's mother is mutating into a china
cabinet and her father is slowly becoming a parrot. The BBC
has survived, in the person of a tattered announcer who carries
around an empty TV chassis and speaks from it to whomever will
listen. There are policemen too, who, fearing a second attack,
direct the non-existent traffic to "keep moving" from an old
car hulk suspended from a large balloon. The nobility is
represented by Lord Fortnum who, to his total disgust, is
changing into an apartment. He is upset because he feels en-
titled by his rank to mutate into a Stately Home, perhaps, or
at least a flat in a fashionable district--but he is becoming
a lowly bed-sitting room.
    Despite the cataclysm and the societal chaos, people carry
on in the behavioral patterns they know best. Penelope is
forced to marry the elderly Captain Bules Martin, whom her
father feels has better prospects than Alan. The father is
made Prime Minister but is soon entirely parrot and gets eaten.
Penelope's baby is finally born; it is a monster. Fortnum
turns into the anticipated bed-sitter at 29 Cul-de-sac Place.
Captain Martin allows Alan to make love to Penelope. This
time her child is healthy. As Penelope, Alan, and the baby
wander into the sunset, a band is playing "God Save Mrs. Ethel
Shroake," who has become Queen by the rules of succession.

Credits:

Director:	Richard Lester
Producers:	Richard Lester, Oscar Lewenstein
	(An Oscar Lewenstein Production)
Associate Producer:	Roy Stevens
Screenplay:	John Antrobus; adapted by Charles
	Wood from the play by Spike Milligan
	and John Antrobus
Photography:	David Watkin (Eastmancolor)
Special Effects:	Phil Stokes
Sound Editor:	Stephen Warwick
Sound Recorder:	Peter Sutton
Sound Re-recorder:	Gerry Humphreys
Music:	Ken Thorne
Production Designer:	Assheton Gorton

Art Director: Michael Seymour
Editor: John Victor Smith
Assistant Director: Richard Burge
Cast: "(in order of size)" Rita Tushingham
                            (Penelope), Dudley Moore (Police Ser-
                            geant), Harry Secombe (Shelter man),
                            Arthur Lowe (Father), Roy Kinnear
                            (Plastic mac man), Spike Milligan
                            (Mate), Ronald Fraser (The Army),
                            Jimmy Edwards (Nigel), Michael Hor-
                            dern (Bules Martin), Peter Cook
                            (Police Inspector), Ralph Richardson
                            (Lord Fortnum, the well-known bed-
                            sitting room), Mona Washbourne
                            (Mother), Richard Warwick (Alan),
                            Frank Thornton (The BBC), Dandy
                            Nichols (Mrs. Ethel Shroake), Jack
                            Shepard (Underwater vicar), and in-
                            troducing Marty Feldman (Nurse Ar-
                            thur); Bill Wallis (The Prime
                            Minister), Henry Woolf (Electricity
                            man), Gordon Rollings (Drip feed
                            patient), Ronald J. Brody (Chauf-
                            feur), Cecil Cheng (Chairman Mao),
                            Eddie Malin (Club waiter), Chris
                            Konyils (Policeman), Clement Freud.
Filmed on location at
a refuse dump in West
Drayton, England.
Distribution: United Artists
Running time: 91 minutes (8,201 feet)
Released: 28 September 1969 (New York City)

11   THE THREE MUSKETEERS   (Panama, 1973)
      (THE QUEEN'S DIAMONDS)

Synopsis:

     The time is the mid-1620's; Louis XIII is King of France
but Cardinal Richelieu has equal power. France is divided into Royalist and Cardinalist camps. Young d'Artagnan leaves
his father's Gascony farm for Paris, hoping to enlist in the
King's Musketeers. He carries a letter of introduction from
his father to Treville, Captain of the Musketeers; his father's
sword; and some of his mother's special ointment. En route he
encounters the Cardinal's chief agent, Rochefort, who is waiting to communicate with his mistress and fellow-spy, Milady de
Winter; d'Artagnan is taunted, assaulted and has his sword
broken by Rochefort's henchmen.
     When he reaches Paris, M. de Treville tells him that he
needs experience and arranges his admission into the King's

Guards. D'Artagnan catches sight of Rochefort, and, hurrying
to intercept him, slams into Athos, who is newly wounded in a
skirmish with some Cardinal's Guards. Athos goads d'Artagnan
into appointing for a duel at noon. Hastening away, the Gascon bumps into Porthos, disarranging his cape and revealing
the plain leather back of the splendid gold baldric he is
wearing. Their duel is set for one o'clock. Finally, d'Artagnan accidentally calls attention to one of Aramis' dalliances,
and they decide to duel at two.

At the convent courtyard where they have agreed to fight,
d'Artagnan has only time to offer Athos some of his mother's
ointment and a three-day postponement of the duel before he
discovers that the latter's seconds are Porthos and Aramis.
The Musketeers are impressed by his audacity. Before he and
Athos cross swords they are interrupted by hostile Cardinal's
Guards, with whom the King's Musketeers maintain a fierce
rivalry. D'Artagnan declines both parties' suggestions that,
as an outsider, he should withdraw, and allies himself with
his erstwhile enemies. The four of them win the ensuing acrobatic duel. Dividing the money Porthos has plundered from one
of the Guards, Athos suggests that d'Artagnan use his share to
find quarters and a servant. Later, clothed in modest splendor
and accompanied by his round and unprepossessing new valet,
Planchet, he asks the innkeeper Bonacieux for a room. The
pigsty he is shown takes on sudden charm when he sees the delicious, clumsy Constance Bonacieux. Her husband explains that
she is the Queen's dressmaker and usually stays at the Palace,
but visits him periodically. That night, Rochefort raids the
Bonacieux house on the Cardinal's hunch that the couple are
conspiring with the Queen, Anne of Austria, and her lover, the
British Duke of Buckingham. Bonacieux is seized but Constance
escapes; she goes to d'Artagnan for solace, which he provides
with alacrity.

When, some time later, Constance goes to the Queen, d'Artagnan follows her. When she surreptitiously meets a nobleman,
the jealous Gascon offers to kill him--until he is revealed to
be Buckingham, on his way to a laundry-room assignation with
Anne. D'Artagnan's services as a bodyguard are enlisted. When
(after a few tender moments and Anne's gift to Buckingham of a
collar of diamond studs) the lovers are betrayed and accosted
by King's Guards, d'Artagnan joins Buckingham in the brawl.
Planchet brings the Musketeers, who fight and win a free-for-
all amid blue dye and soapy water. Buckingham returns to England. The Cardinal, learning from a traitorous lady-in-waiting
of Anne's gift, persuades the King to give a ball at which Anne
will wear the studs, which had been the King's gift to her.
Constance promises to get a message to Buckingham at the same
time that Richelieu orders Milady to steal two of the studs.

At first Constance plans to send her husband, but he has
been subverted during a stay at the Bastille and is now an
avid Cardinalist. D'Artagnan volunteers and enlists the aid

of the Musketeers. Along the way Porthos, Athos, and Aramis are wounded and left behind. D'Artagnan encounters Rochefort at the seaport and they fight. The Gascon wins and, taking Rochefort's paper of passage, sails for England. He reaches Buckingham, who only now discovers the theft of the two studs by Milady during a dalliance. A jeweler quickly manufactures two more studs; d'Artagnan and Planchet race back to France. On the way to Paris they appropriate a fresh horse outside an inn, cutting it loose from a rope which is, unknown to them, currently being used by the debilitated Porthos and Aramis to pull the equally debilitated and drunken Athos out of a well. Recognizing him in passing by his "unfortunate accent," the Musketeers follow him to Paris in sedan chairs.

D'Artagnan arrives at the Palace during the ball; the studs are already missed, and the Cardinal has presented the stolen ones to the confused King. D'Artagnan is momentarily prevented from delivering the studs by Cardinal's men; but his friends arrive and he has a chance to throw the bundle through the Palace window. After a scuffle with Milady, Constance gives the collar to the Queen. The presence of all twelve studs thwarts the Cardinal.

During a day of chivalric games presided over by the bored King and grateful Queen, d'Artagnan is made a Musketeer by the rather apprehensive Treville. As he leaves with his friends and Constance, the relentless Richelieu, Rochefort, and Milady are seen lurking ominously in the background.

Credits:

Director:	Richard Lester
Producer:	Alexander Salkind (Film Trust S. A.)
Executive Producer:	Ilya Salkind
Associate Executive Producer:	Pierre Spengler
Screenplay:	George MacDonald Fraser, based on the novel by Alexandre Dumas père.
Photography:	David Watkin (Technicolor)
Second Unit Director and Photographer	Paul Wilson
Special Effects:	Eddie Fowlie; supervisor, Pablo Perez
Sound Editors:	Don Sharpe, Don Challis
Sound Recorders:	Simon Kaye, Roy J. Charman
Sound Re-recorder:	Gerry Humphreys
Music:	Michel Legrand
Production Designer:	Brian Eatwell
Art Directors:	Les Dilley, Fernando Gonzalez
Editor:	John Victor Smith
Titles:	Camera Effects
Swordmaster/Fight Arranger:	William Hobbs
Stunts:	Arranged by Joaquin Parra

Production Manager:	Francisco Bellot
Production Supervisor:	Enrique Esteban
Production Coordinator:	Jean-Phillipe Merand
Assistant Director:	Clive Reed
Continuity:	Anne Skinner
Makeup:	Jose Antonio Sanchez
Costumes:	Yvonne Blake; Raquel Welch's costumes by Ron Talsky
Cast:	Michael York (d'Artagnan), Oliver Reed (Athos), Raquel Welch (Constance Bonacieux), Richard Chamberlain (Aramis), Frank Finlay (Porthos/ O'Reilly), Charlton Heston (Cardinal Richelieu), Faye Dunaway (Milady de Winter), Christopher Lee (Rochefort), Geraldine Chaplin (Anne of Austria), Jean-Pierre Cassel (Louis XIII), Spike Milligan (M. Bonacieux), Roy Kinnear (Planchet), Michael Gothard (Felton), Sybil Danning (Eugenie), Gitty Djamal (Beatrice), Simon Ward (Duke of Buckingham), Nicole Calfan (Kitty), Georges Wilson (Captain de Treville), Angel Del Pozo (Jussac), Rodney Bewes (Richelieu's spy), Ben Aris (First Musketeer), Joss Ackland (d'Artagnan's father), Gretchen Franklyn (d'Artagnan's mother), Francis de Wolff (Captain), William Hobbs (Swordsman at inn).

Filmed on location in Spain (after red tape in Hungary, the original location, proved insurmountable).

Distribution:	20th Century-Fox/Rank
Running time:	107 minutes (9,587 feet)
Released:	25 March 1974 (London: Royal Performance)

12   JUGGERNAUT   (U.S.A., 1974)

Synopsis:

As the luxury liner Britannic sails, the steamship company officials receive a bomb threat from someone calling himself Juggernaut. He says there are seven bombs on the ship which will explode unless he receives £500,000 ransom. He has timed one of the bombs to go off at the end of his call, to demonstrate his sincerity.

The steamship company advises the ship's captain to sail in circles and evade the passengers' questions about the first, nearly harmless, blast. The bombs cannot be moved; the ship is too far out at sea to return, and the storms and choppy waters make rescue of the 1200 people on board by air or lifeboat impossible. Although the steamship company wants to pay the ransom, the government, who subsidizes it, wants to discourage further terrorism and says Juggernaut should not be paid.

Scotland Yard is put onto the task of finding Juggernaut. In charge is Superintendent John McCleod, whose disillusioned American wife and children are on the <u>Britannic</u>, cruising to the States for what is less a vacation than an estrangement. Part of his wife's disenchantment with him results from his reputation for plea-bargaining with petty crooks in order to snag bigger ones. After an attempt to trace Juggernaut's second call fails, McCleod resorts to this tactic again while interviewing jailed bomb experts about Juggernaut's possible identity. No one he talks to can, or will, help him. The Yard continues to sift through its list of bomb experts.

It is decided to send a Naval bomb disposal team to the <u>Brittanic</u>. The team, headed by Tony Fallon and his right-hand man Charlie Braddock, are parachuted into the choppy waters near the liner. They see that the bombs, in large barrels, are fiendishly placed to do maximum damage and probably booby-trapped at the bolted-on plate covering the hole used to install the works. After sandbagging the bomb areas as much as possible, Fallon's team divides itself among the bombs, keeping in touch with Fallon by radio. He realizes that the bombs are clever, but that his biggest problem is trying to outguess the bomber. Should he, for instance, look for booby-traps in out-of-the-ordinary places, or should he assume that Juggernaut knows that any disposal expert would try the hard places first, and so booby-trap the easy ones? The war of nerves continues as Fallon successfully opens his barrel. However, the other barrels still hold secrets which cost the lives of some of his team.

The passengers and crew, meanwhile, have been informed and are bearing up surprisingly well. Mr. Curtain, the social director, valiantly tries to raise spirits; he receives unexpected help from Barbara Bannister, a passenger who is the Captain's mistress for this voyage. Their efforts enliven, at least a little, a dance party that has all the gaiety of Death Row. The imminence of death causes a middle-aged couple--an amiable, corrupt American mayor and his wife--to rediscover their love. One of the ship's stewards, Azad, sacrifices himself to save McCleod's son from a bomb which is triggered accidentally.

Fallon is badly shaken when Braddock touches a trip-wire and is blown up. He gets drunk with the Captain as they wait for events to develop.

The steamship company head has raised the ransom, despite the government's disapproval. However, Juggernaut's contact is apprehended after collecting the money. McCleod's team soon learns who Juggernaut is: he is Buckland, Fallon's old mentor who, lacking imagination and daring, has remained an embittered, underpaid public servant.

Fallon, knowing that the bombs have myriad tricks in them that will make it impossible for his team to disarm them in time, demands to speak to Buckland over the radio. There are two wires; the right move will secure the ship, the wrong one will destroy it. He asks Buckland which wire to cut. Buckland tells him to cut the blue wire. In a final psychological analysis, Fallon realizes that Buckland is bitter enough to destroy the ship anyway. He cuts the red wire and the ship is saved.

Credits:

Director:	Richard Lester
Producer:	Richard de Koker (United Artists)
Executive Producer:	David V. Picker
Associate Producer:	Denis O'Dell
Screenplay:	Richard de Koker; additional dialogue by Alan Plater
Photography:	Gerry Fisher (Panavision; color by DeLuxe)
Second Unit Photography:	Paul Wilson
Aerial Photographer:	Peter Allwork
Special Effects:	Cliff Richardson, John Richardson, Joe Fitt
Sound Recorders:	Simon Kaye, Gerry Humphreys
Sound Re-recorder:	Les Wiggins
Music:	Ken Thorne
Production Designer:	Terence Marsh
Art Directors:	Alan Tomkins, George Richardson
Set Decorator:	Ian Whittaker
Editor:	Antony Gibbs
Production Manager:	Roy Stevens
Assistant Directors:	David Tringham, Terry Hodgkinson, Vincent Winter
Technical Consultant:	Lt. Comm. Sidney Walton
Cast:	Richard Harris (Fallon), Omar Sharif (The Captain), David Hemmings (Charlie Braddock), Anthony Hopkins (Supt. John McCleod), Ian Holm (Nicholas Porter), Shirley Knight (Barbara), Roy Kinnear (Social director, Mr. Curtain), Roshan Seth (Azad), Cyril Cusack (O'Neill, bomb expert in prison), Freddie Jones (Sid Buckland), Kristine Howarth (Mrs. Buckland), Clifton James

(Corrigan), Mark Burns (First Offi-
cer Hollingsworth), Gareth Thomas
(Second officer), Andrew Bradford
(Third officer), Richard Moore
(Junior officer), Jack Watson (Chief
Engineer Mallicent), Bob Sessions
(Jerry Kellog), Liza Ross (Laura
Kellog), Michael Egan (Mr. Fowlers),
Ben Aris (The walker), Paul Antrim
(Digby), Colin Thatcher (Henning),
Terence Hillyer (Menzies), John
Stride (Hughes), Michael Hordern
(Baker), Norman Warwick (Bartender),
Freddie Fletcher (Second radio offi-
cer), John Bindon (Driscoll), Caro-
line Mortimer (Susan McCleod), Adam
Bridge (David McCleod), Rebecca
Bridge (Nancy McCleod), Julian Glo-
ver (Commander Marder), Kenneth
Colley (Detective Brown), Tom Chad-
bon (Juggernaut contact), Kenneth
Cope (Bridgeman), Barnaby Holm
(Christopher Porter), Victor Lewis
(Detective), Paul Luty (Clerk),
Simon MacCorkindale (No. 1 helmsman),
Eric Mason (Second detective),
Michael Melia (Navigator), Rosamund
Nelson (Clerk at air terminal), Doris
Nolan (Mrs. Corrigan), John Penning-
ton (Passenger), David Purcell (First
detective), Martin Read (Kelsey),
Howard Southern (Detective Skinner),
Ian Talbot (Naval technician).

Filmed on location
aboard the Soviet
liner Maxim Gorki.
Distribution: United Artists
Running time: 110 minutes (9,888 feet)
Released: September 1974 (Los Angeles)

13   THE FOUR MUSKETEERS   (Panama/Spain, 1973)
      (THE REVENGE OF MILADY)

Synopsis:

    Louis XIII and his Musketeers are engaged in trying to sup-
press the Protestants at the siege of La Rochelle. Athos,
Porthos, and Aramis rescue their old enemy Rochefort from the
Huguenots, on whom he has been spying. The King (who wishes
to stop his wife's consorting with the Duke of Buckingham) and

Richelieu instruct Rochefort to kidnap Anne's go-between, Constance Bonacieux. She is in Paris with her fledgling Musketeer, d'Artagnan, when she is seized in the marketplace. D'Artagnan is assaulted and knocked out by a cart full of potatoes and recovers in the chamber of Rochefort's mistress, Milady de Winter, who has been instructed to keep him busy. Although attracted by Milady, he is upset at Constance's disappearance. Confiding in a more than usually drunken Athos, he receives in return the latter's thinly disguised story of his former life. He had been the Comte de la Fére, a rich, honorable man who had fallen in love with a girl of mean birth. Instead of wantoning her, he had married her. One day he had discovered that she had been branded with a fleur-de-lis, the mark of a criminal. She had turned on him and he, enraged at her deception and the dishonor to his family, had (he thought) strangled her. (He is mistaken; unknown to himself and d'Artagnan, the former Comtesse de la Fére is now Milady de Winter.)

D'Artagnan, learning of Milady's complicity in Constance's abduction, has the ill-luck to confront her with this knowledge while they are in bed; during the ensuing dust-up he sees the fleur-de-lis on her shoulder. He escapes with his skin and a necklace pulled off in the scuffle. Later, seeing this bauble, Athos identifies it as one he had given his own lady. Knowing her viciousness, he fruitlessly advises d'Artagnan to remove himself from her reach.

The Cardinal offers d'Artagnan a place in his own Guards. The refusal is taken with equanimity, but Richelieu warns/ threatens him that his future survival at La Rochelle will be precarious, and not just because of the war. As d'Artagnan rides to La Rochelle, his friends rescue Constance, leaving her at a convent for safekeeping, and then head for the front themselves. When the Gascon arrives, he finds a gift of wine allegedly from the three others. On his way to meet them so they can all drink it together, d'Artagnan is ambushed by Rochefort and his men. His friends, as usual, arrive at an opportune moment, as d'Artagnan duels Rochefort on an icy river. The four take one of Rochefort's men prisoner; from him they learn of suspicious doings at an inn called the Red Dovecote. They pour him some of the gift wine, he dies, and Athos, Porthos, and Aramis deny any knowledge of the wine.

The three of them go to the Red Dovecote and are surprised when Richelieu himself turns up. Athos decides to eavesdrop and the others leave for the front to keep an eye on d'Artagnan. Athos overhears Richelieu's orders to Milady—she is to prevent Buckingham from aiding the Protestants at all costs. In return she demands the deaths of d'Artagnan and Constance. For this purpose he gives her a discreet, noncommital carte blanche: "...for the good of the state, the bearer has done what has been done." Before Milady can leave, Athos confronts her, simultaneously relieving her of the carte blanche and issuing an unmistakeable warning against harming d'Artagnan.

Returning to the front, he engineers a breakfast at the only unwatched spot around--a ruined bastion near the Protestant lines which the King's forces have been trying to take and hold. The four and the reluctant Planchet hold the fort as they eat; Athos gives d'Artagnan the carte blanche and tells him of the danger to Buckingham. D'Artagnan is able to warn the Queen but can't go to Buckingham unobserved, so he sends Planchet. Meanwhile, Milady has failed to dissuade Buckingham and plans to kill him. He has her arrested before she can try, and puts her in the custody of an implacable Puritan, Felton, whom she quickly seduces. At her bidding he frees her and assassinates Buckingham just as Planchet reaches him with Anne's warning.

Back in France, La Rochelle has fallen to the King. The Musketeers ride to collect Constance, but on the way they discover that Milady and Rochefort have the same idea. The two parties arrive at the convent simultaneously. During the ensuing brawl. Milady dresses as a nun and strangles the unsuspecting Constance with a rosary. D'Artagnan finds the body and searches for Rochefort, who has disappeared after fighting with Athos. They duel inside the cathedral; d'Artagnan kills Rochefort and collapses, exhausted. Athos has, meanwhile, prevented Milady's escape. Later the four Musketeers, holding court on a quiet wooded riverbank, try her and find her guilty. Athos, who as a count can dispense justice, orders her death at the hands of an executioner hired for the purpose. This is done as they bleakly look on.

The four are arrested by the Cardinal's men and d'Artagnan is brought before Richelieu. He answers the charges against him by presenting the Cardinal's own anonymous carte blanche. With a rueful "one must be careful of what one writes," Richelieu frees him and gives him a blank commission for a lieutenancy in the Musketeers. He offers it to each of his friends, who decline it, telling him he's earned it himself.

Credits:

Director:	Richard Lester
Producers:	Alexander Salkind, Michael Salkind (Film Trust, Panama/Este Films, Madrid)
Executive Producer:	Ilya Salkind
Associate Producer:	Wolfdieter von Stein
Associate Executive Producer:	Pierre Spengler
Screenplay:	George MacDonald Fraser from the novel The Three Musketeers by Alexandre Dumas père.
Photography:	David Watkin (Technicolor; prints by DeLuxe)
Second Unit Director and Photographer:	Paul Wilson

Special Effects:	Eddie Fowlie; supervised by Pablo Perez
Sound Editors:	Don Sharpe, Don Challis
Sound Recorders:	Simon Kaye, Roy J. Charman
Sound Re-recorder:	Gerry Humphreys
Music:	Lalo Schifrin
Production Designer:	Brian Eatwell
Art Directors:	Les Dilley, Fernando Gonzalez
Editor:	John Victor Smith
Titles:	Camera Effects
Swordmaster/Fight Arranger:	William Hobbs
Stunts:	Arranged by Joaquin Parra
Production Manager:	Francisco Bellot
Production Supervisor:	Enrique Esteban
Production Coordinator:	Jean-Phillipe Merand
Assistant Directors:	Clive Reed, Dusty Symonds, Francisco Rodriguez, Patricio Beltran Apario, Alain Walk
Continuity:	Anne Skinner
Makeup:	Jose Antonio Sanchez
Costumes:	Yvonne Blake; Raquel Welch's costumes by Ron Talsky
Cast:	Oliver Reed (Athos), Raquel Welch (Constance Bonacieux), Richard Chamberlain (Aramis), Michael York (d'Artagnan), Frank Finlay (Porthos), Simon Ward (Duke of Buckingham), Christopher Lee (Rochefort), Faye Dunaway (Milady de Winter), Charlton Heston (Cardinal Richelieu), Geraldine Chaplin (Anne of Austria), Jean-Pierre Cassel (Louis XIII), Roy Kinnear (Planchet), Nicole Calfan (Kitty), Eduardo Fajardo (General), Michael Gothard (Felton), Sybil Danning (Eugenie), Gitty Djamal (Beatrice), Angel Del Pozo (Jussac), Leon Greene (Swiss Guard officer), Norman Chappell (Submarine inventor), Lucy Tiller (Mother Superior), Tyrone Cassidy (English officer), Jack Watson (Busigny), Tom Buchanan (Firing squad sergeant), Bob Todd (Firing squad officer), Richard Adams (Tortured thug).

Filmed on location in Spain.

Distribution:	20th Century-Fox/Rank
Running time:	103 minutes (9,234 feet)
Released:	19 March 1975 (New York City)

14   ROYAL FLASH   (Great Britain, 1975)

Synopsis:

Captain Harry Flashman has gained fame as a hero of the Afghanistan wars by dint of having singlehandedly defended the British flag against the enemy at a garrison they were overrunning. As he jingoistically and inspirationally addresses his old school, Rugby, a flashback reveals that the reason he was found unconscious, protecting the flag with his body, was that he had stumbled while rushing out to surrender it. In fact, his entire career has been based on his betters' inability to discover his acts of cowardice. He has used this to advantage, in terms of both prestige and money, and is able to maintain a typically dissolute Victorian lifestyle. One night the gambling club he frequents is raided. In a room upstairs, a game of mixed-doubles strip poker has reached the moment of truth but the commotion downstairs obliges its participants, one of whom is Harry, to flee. Harry runs through the London streets just far enough ahead of a policeman to dart into a carriage and pretend to be the companion of the woman within-- who, surprisingly, backs him up. She is the infamous Lola Montes. However, her actual companion is angered by Flashman's bourgeois insolence, and nearly has him arrested. This young gentleman is the up-and-coming Otto von Bismarck. He is further aggravated by Lola's decision to take Harry home with her instead of him. His growing dislike of Flashman is increased when, at a soirée, Harry goads him into a boxing match with the former British champion, John Gully. Bismarck behaves arrogantly and fights dirty, but he is nonetheless trounced, humiliated and relieved of a tooth. Soon afterward, Flashman and Lola part company; Lola is in trouble for duelling with a soprano, and besides, Harry finds himself unequal to her penchant for hitting him with a hairbrush in bed.
Four years pass, and Harry is unexpectedly summoned to Bavaria by Lola, who is the mad King Ludwig's mistress. At a large party, Harry and Lola arrange a rendezvous. Flashman goes to an exotic bedroom and pounces on what he thinks is Lola. It turns out to be a hefty baroness who nearly ravishes _him_, then cries rape. Her incensed male relatives tie him to a butcher's table in the kitchen and prepare to neuter him. At the last moment the slick Hungarian mercenary Rudi von Starnberg swashbuckles to the rescue. Harry doesn't suspect that he has been set up until Rudi brings him to the hold of Schonhausen and he comes face to face with its squire--Bismarck. The latter tells him that he has been brought there to help ease a painful political situation. An advantageous marriage between the heads of two German states is threatened, and with it the unification of Germany that Bismarck desires. The groom, Crown Prince Karl, has contracted venereal disease; the cure will prevent his marrying Princess Irma of Strackenz on schedule. Flashman bears a striking resemblance to Karl;

45

Bismarck proposes that he impersonate the groom until the cure takes effect, and makes it clear that Harry has no choice but to agree. Harry agrees.

Bismarck and Rudi drill Harry relentlessly until he masters Karl's mannerisms and knows what is expected of him. A few alterations are made in his appearance. These include the addition of two Heidelberg-style facial duelling scars, which Bismarck personally inflicts.

The wedding goes smoothly, with Bismarck and Rudi close by in case of emergency. Only a former close friend of Karl's, Eric Hansen, realizes there is anything wrong; he is quickly and quietly killed. That night, Harry finds that Irma is a sexual icicle, but by using his usual method of "treating 'em hearty," he reduces her to slavish adoration and insatiable erotic appetite within a few hours.

Almost immediately he goes hunting with some of Bismarck's henchmen, who try to kill him. He manages to escape and to find out that Bismarck's real plan is to kill both Flashman and Karl (whom he has kidnapped) and to seize power. Harry takes to the hills, only to be captured by the patriotic guerrilla Volsungs, who force him to help them rescue the real Karl. To his own amazement and everyone else's, he does so; luckily, Flashman's frantic efforts to save his own neck work to Karl's advantage as well. These include treacherously knocking out Rudi during a friendly conversation. Rudi wakes up in time to fight a grudge duel with Harry; however, realizing that Bismarck's game is up, he leaves the fight unresolved and flees before the Volsungs can get him.

Flashman hurries back to Strackenz to bid Irma goodbye (wondering in passing whether Karl will be equal to replacing him) and to steal as many of the crown jewels as he can carry. Retracing his route back to England, he encounters Lola, who is being expelled by the irate Bavarians. He begs passage in her lavish travelling coach, and she agrees when she sees his loot. After a night of love Flashman awakes in the deserted coach in the middle of nowhere; a note from Lola replaces his plunder. He is discovered thus by Rudi, who has cut his losses and left Bismarck. They begin to philosophize as they sip wine in the carriage, and pass the time by playing a game Rudi has devised: he calls it "Hungarian roulette." The game continues until Harry, discovering that the gun they've been fooling with is loaded, bleats "I could've been killed!"

Credits:

Director:	Richard Lester
Producers:	David V. Picker and Denis O'Dell (Two Roads Production)
Screenplay:	George MacDonald Fraser from his own novel
Photography:	Geoffrey Unsworth (Technicolor; prints by DeLuxe)

Second Unit Photography: Paul Wilson
Special Effects: John Richardson
Sound Editors: Don Sharpe, Paul Smith
Sound Recorders: Simon Kaye, Gerry Humphreys
Music: Adapted and directed by Ken Thorne
Production Designer: Terence Marsh
Art Director: Alan Tomkins
Construction: Peter Dukelow
Editor: John Victor Smith
Fight Director: William Hobbs
Stunts: Arranged by Richard Graydon
Production Manager: Barry Melrose (Germany), Hubert Froehlich
Assistant Directors: Vincent Winter, Dusty Symonds
Unit Manager: Brian Burgess
Casting: Mary Selway
Continuity: Anne Skinner
Costumes: Alan Barrett
Cast: Malcolm McDowell (Captain Harry Flashman/Crown Prince Karl), Alan Bates (Rudi von Starnberg), Florinda Bolkan (Lola Montes), Britt Ekland (Duchess Irma of Strackenz), Oliver Reed (Otto von Bismarck), Lionel Jeffries (Kraftstein), Tom Bell (De Gautet), Christopher Cazenove (Eric Hansen), Joss Ackland (Sapten), Leon Greene (Grundwig), Richard Hurndall (Detchard), Alastair Sim (Mr. Greig), Michael Hordern (Headmaster), Roy Kinnear (Old Roue), David Stern (Policeman), Richard Pearson (Josef), Rula Lenska (Helga), Margaret Courtenay (Soprano), Noel Johnson (Lord Chamberlain), Elizabeth Larner (Baroness Pechman), Henry Cooper (John Gully), Stuart Rayner (Speedicutt), Ben Aris (Fireman), Bob Peck (Police inspector), John Stuart (English General), Frank Grimes (Lieutenant), Paul Burton (Tom Brown), Tessa Dahl (First girl), Claire Russell (Second girl), Kubi Choza (Lucy), Meg Davies (Barmaid), Roger Hammond (Master), David Jason (Mayor), Alan Howard, Bob Hoskins, Arthur Brough.

Filmed on location in Germany.
Distribution: 20th Century-Fox/Rank
Running time: 118 minutes (10,641 feet)
Released: 11 July 1975 (London)

15   ROBIN AND MARIAN   (U.S.A., 1976)

Synopsis:

The year is 1199. Richard the Lion-Heart and the remainder
of his army, among whom are Robin Hood and Little John, are
finally returning from the Holy Land after twenty years. They
stop at the castle of Chaluz, where Richard demands the treasure that supposedly lies there. The old man who is the castle's
sole defender denies that there is a treasure, but the mostly-
mad Richard orders the castle razed. Robin and John refuse to
obey and are arrested. The old man throws an arrow which
freakishly wounds Richard in the neck. Nevertheless he de-
stroys the castle and the women and children left in it. There
is no treasure. He has his wound treated and plans to deal
with Robin and John in the morning. Those two, locked in an
old wine cellar, work all night to escape. Just as they are
about to succeed, Richard sends for them. He is in a bad way;
the arrow wound is killing him and he's no longer disposed to
kill Robin and John. He dies in Robin's arms.

As Richard's casket is borne away to burial in France,
Robin and John decide to return to England and Sherwood.
Months later they arrive, to find it much overgrown and rather
unfamiliar. They can barely find their old camp, until they
are ambushed by two old men who turn out to be Friar Tuck and
Will Scarlett. The others have all gone away or died. However, the Sheriff is still ruling Nottingham, and King John
the usurper is perpetrating worse deeds than ever. Will suggests that Robin is still needed and could easily raise a
following if he decided to fight the King again. Robin dismisses the idea but begins to warm to it, and to the thought
of seeing Marian, whom he says he hasn't thought about in
years.

The four of them ride to Kirkly, near Nottingham, to see
Marian. Will and Tuck then reveal that she has been a nun for
eighteen years and is now Abbess at Kirkly Abbey. Her recep-
tion of Robin is, to say the least, unenthusiastic. She is
harried because she is expecting to be arrested at any moment,
King John having ordered all the higher clergy out of England
and she having refused to leave. Robin's offer of help is
snappishly rejected. Nevertheless, he rescues her from the
Sheriff and his aide, Sir Ranulf, much against her will, and
carries her off to Sherwood. Ranulf is hot for Robin's blood,
but the Sheriff is almost regretful as he realizes he has to
kill him.

Marian, despite Robin's returning affection for her, determines to turn herself in to the Sheriff. Back at Kirkly, she
finds that the Sheriff and Ranulf have seized three of her
nuns in lieu of her. Robin sees this as the Sheriff's tactic
to trap him. He sends Marian back to Sherwood with Will and
Tuck while he and John, disguised as peddlers, go to

Nottingham. The Sheriff recognizes them immediately and has the captive nuns brought into the city square for exercise. The outlaws tell the nuns to run to the wagon they have waiting outside the gate. They escape just as the portcullis descends, leaving Robin and John to climb it and wage a strenuous fight on the battlements. At last reinforcements, in the form of Will, Tuck, and Marian, arrive and turn the tide of the skirmish, and all escape to Sherwood again.

The old lovers find it progressively easier to fall back into love. As they sit alone by a stream, Marian confesses that when Robin had left, all those years ago, she had tried suicide. She had been carried to Kirkly and had stayed there. Their idyll is interrupted by the news that Sir Ranulf's men have come after them. Robin and John ride to tell Ranulf to clear off, and rout his men. Marian prepares to live in Sherwood. The five are joined by men from the villages who want to fight at Robin's side.

Ranulf goes to King John with a demand for men to combat those who are joining Robin in droves. John gives him the men and puts pressure on the Sheriff to get Robin.

The Sheriff camps near the forest and waits for Robin to come out, and because he expects it, Robin comes out. Marian has pleaded with him and John not to go, knowing they'll lose, and has threatened to leave. Robin and the Sheriff agree to fight one-to-one, the stakes being the safety of Robin's band. As the fight begins, Marian is returning to Kirkly, but finds herself running toward the battlefield instead.

The fight has remained fairly even, but both men are bleeding and winded. Finally the Sheriff finds an opening and plunges his sword into Robin's side. As he falls, Robin runs the Sheriff through the chest. Sir Ranulf, unwilling to keep the Sheriff's bargain, heads a charge against Robin's waiting men. The infuriated John kills him and, as the battle moves into Sherwood, he and Marian help Robin to the Abbey where her medicines are. As John keeps watch outside, Marian mixes a potion, tastes it and gives it to Robin. Knowing he has survived worse wounds, he plans to resume the old glorious life as soon as possible. He begins to be troubled by numbness in his legs, but it is only when he sees Marian having similar problems that he realizes that she has poisoned them both.

After a first panicked outcry, Robin accepts the situation, knowing after all that his best days are past. As the poison spreads, he tells John, who has come at his cry, to bring him his bow and an arrow. Shooting it through the window, he says that he and Marian are to be buried where it lands.

Credits:

Director:	Richard Lester
Producers:	Richard Shepherd and Denis O'Dell
	(Rastar, for Columbia)

49

Executive Producer:	Ray Stark
Screenplay:	James Goldman
Photography:	David Watkin (Technicolor)
Second Unit Photography:	Paul Wilson
Cameraman:	Jim Turrell
Special Effects:	Eddie Fowlie
Sound Editors:	Don Sharp, Paul Smith
Sound Recorders:	Roy Charman, Gerry Humphreys
Music:	John Barry
Music Editor:	Michael Clifford
Production Designer:	Michael Stringer
Art Director:	Gil Parrando
Property Master:	Francisco Prosper
Editor:	John Victor Smith
Assistant Editor:	Peter Boyle
Fight Directors:	William Hobbs, Ian McKay
Stunt Arrangers:	Miguel Pedregosa, Joaquin Parra
Production Manager:	Apolinar Rabinal
Production Supervisors and Co-ordinators:	Barrie Melrose, Roberto Roberts
Assistant Director:	Jose Lopez Rodero
Unit Managers:	Dusty Symonds, Juan Clemente
Casting:	Mary Selway
Script:	Ann Skinner
Makeup:	Jose Antonio Sanchez
Costumes:	Yvonne Blake
Cast:	Sean Connery (Robin Hood), Audrey Hepburn (Maid Marian), Robert Shaw (Sheriff of Nottingham), Richard Harris (King Richard the Lion-Heart), Nicol Williamson (Little John), Denholm Elliott (Will Scarlett), Kenneth Haigh (Sir Ranulf de Pudsey), Ronnie Barker (Friar Tuck), Ian Holm (King John), Bill Maynard (Mercadier), Esmond Knight (Old defender), Veronica Quilligan (Sister Mary), Peter Butterworth (Surgeon), John Barrett (Jack), Kenneth Cranham (Jack's apprentice), Victoria Merida Roja (Queen Isabella), Montserrat Julio (First sister), Victoria Hernandez Sanguino (Second sister), Marguerita Manguillon (Third sister).
Filmed on location in Spain.	
Distribution:	Columbia/Warner
Running time:	107 minutes (9,608 feet)
Released:	11 March 1976 (New York City)

16   THE RITZ   (Great Britain, 1976)

Synopsis:

   Papa Vespucci's dying words to his son Carmine are "Get
Proclo!" Dutifully, Carmine sets out to kill his despised
brother-in-law, Gaetano Proclo, the timid owner of a garbage
collection firm in Cleveland. Proclo, wearing an improbable
disguise, flees to Manhattan, where he instructs a cab driver
to take him someplace where no one will think to look for him;
the knowing cabby drops him at the Ritz, a bath house for gay
males. The unsuspecting Proclo signs in despite the odd residents who file past. Inside, he encounters Chris, who is looking for a date; Claude, a "chubby chasing" Army acquaintance
who keeps trying to get Proclo into his room to ply him with
food; Googie Gomez, a questionable singer who has been told
Proclo is a big producer (and whom Proclo assumes is a trans-
vestite); and Michael Brick, a baby-faced, squeaky-voiced
would-be Bogart private eye hired by Carmine to find Proclo.
Brick has never seen either Proclo or Carmine before, and
takes Gaetano for Carmine, whom he has arranged to meet--while
Carmine takes Chris for Brick. A multiple chase ensues, during
which Carmine finds Proclo, Googie, and Chris hiding under a
bed and assumes he has caught them in flagrante delicto. Brick
knocks him out and the chase resumes, with the added element
of Vivian, Proclo's wife, who has come to try to dissuade her
brother from killing him.
   As the time for the poolside talent show approaches, Claude
persuades Proclo to help him revive their old Army routine, an
Andrews Sisters impression, with Chris as the third. Carmine,
professing outrage at finding his brother-in-law at such a
dive, orders everyone into the pool and is prepared to kill
Proclo when the Ritz's bookkeeper reveals that the supposedly
devout Vespucci family owns the bath house. Vivian forces
Carmine to withdraw his contract on Gaetano by threatening to
leak this information to another Mafia family. The Proclos
leave, Gaetano with a talent show trophy; Carmine, who has
been forced into a dress by his vengeful relatives, is arrested.

Credits:

Director:	Richard Lester
Producer:	Denis O'Dell (Courtyard Films for Warner Brothers)
Screenplay:	Terence McNally, from his own play
Photography:	Paul Wilson (Technicolor)
Special Effects:	Colin Chilvers
Sound Editor:	Don Sharpe
Sound Recorders:	Roy Charman, Gerry Humphreys
Music:	Composed, directed and arranged by Ken Thorne

Songs:	Sung by C. T. Wilkinson
Production Designer:	Philip Harrison
Editor:	John Bloom
Stunts:	Staged by Paul Weston
Production Manager:	Barrie Melrose
Assistant Director:	Dusty Symonds
Makeup:	Paul Rabiger
Costumes:	Vangie Harrison
Cast:	Jack Weston (Gaetano Proclo), Rita Moreno (Googie Gomez), Jerry Stiller (Carmine Vespucci), Kaye Ballard (Vivian Proclo), Treat Williams (Michael Brick), F. Murray Abraham (Chris), George Coulouris (Papa Vespucci), Paul B. Price (Claude), John Everson (Tiger), Christopher J. Brown (Duff), Dave King (Abe), Bessie Love (Maurine), Tony de Santis (Sheldon Farenholt), Ben Aris (Patron with bicycle), Peter Butterworth (Patron in chaps), Ronnie Brody (Small patron), Hal Gallili (Patron with cigar), John Ratzpenberger (Patron), Chris Harris (Patron), Leon Greene (Muscle-bound patron), Freddie Earle (Disgruntled patron), Hugh Fraser (Disc jockey), Bart Allison (Old Priest), Samantha Weyson (Gilda Proclo), Richard Holmes (Pianist).

Filmed at Twickenham Studios, England.

Distribution:	Columbia-Warner
Running time:	91 minutes (8,162 feet)

Writings about Richard Lester, 1960-1977

1960

17 BROUGHTON, JAMES. "Running, Jumping and Standing Still Film."
    Film Quarterly, 13 (Spring), 57.
        Ideas are "determinedly whimsical," but lack the "attack
    of a creator with wits" to give the film an edge.

*18 SEGUIN, LOUIS. "Running, Jumping and Standing Still." Posi-
    tif, No. 38.
        [Cited in Eyquem, no. 446.]

1962

19 COLEMAN, JOHN. Review of It's Trad, Dad. New Statesman, 63
    (6 April), 501.
        Film starts energetically, but "even Mr. Lester...is
    finally bested by his intractable subject."

1963

20 ANON. "Lunar Buffoonery." Time, 81 (21 June), 92.
        Review of The Mouse on the Moon says Sellers is "sorely
    missed"; some of the humor is tasteless; it is "sparse
    farce."

21 ANON. "Lunar Lunacy." Newsweek, 62 (1 July), 68.
        Describes plot of The Mouse on the Moon.

22 ANON. "The Mouse on the Moon." Filmfacts, 6 (22 August),
    167-68.
        Credits, synopsis, excerpts from popular press reviews.

23 ANON. "The Mouse on the Moon." The Times [London] (2 May),
    p. 6.
        Gags are "silly" but "endearing," resulting in a piece
    of "strangely likeable...British rubbish."

1963

24 CROWTHER, BOSLEY. "The Mouse on the Moon." New York Times
        (18 June), p. 32.
            Film is "delightful," script "droll." The "erratic" di-
        rection enhances it.

25 DURGNAT, RAYMOND. "Mouse on the Moon." Films and Filming, 9
        (June), 29.
            Lester manages some nice satiric thrusts, but film's tone
        is generally "gentle."

26 KENNEY, ANN D. "Mouse on the Moon." Parents' Magazine, 38
        (August), 16.
            Notice; film is "laugh a minute."

27 KNIGHT, ARTHUR. Notice of The Mouse on the Moon. Saturday
        Review, 46 (20 July), 37.
            Movie promises more than it delivers; its impetus is lost
        long before the end.

28 M., M. "Mouse on the Moon." Christian Science Monitor
        [Eastern edition], 55 (10 July), 4.
            Film is softer than The Mouse That Roared, Sellers's
        absence making the prime difference.

29 RICH. "Mouse on the Moon." Variety, 230 (15 May), 6.
            Satire of The Mouse that Roared is absent here, blunted
        by farcical approach. Peter Sellers is missed.

                              1964

30 ANON. "A Hard Day's Night." Filmfacts, 7 (2 October), 196-99.
            Credits, synopsis, excerpts from popular press reviews.

31 ANON. "A Hard Day's Night." [BFI] Monthly Film Bulletin, 31
        (August), 121.
            Credits, synopsis, mini-review which finds the Beatles
        too inexperienced to "make the most of" the frantically-
        paced script. Direction is engaging in spots and fresh
        despite its New Wave origins.

32 ANON. "Off-beat Film on Beatles." The Times [London] (7
        July), p. 15.
            Many of Lester's "bright ideas" come off well in A Hard
        Day's Night--use of music in a non-set-piece way, goonish
        humor, etc.; however, film is too cluttered with gags for
        each to be effective. Actors aren't handled as well as
        they could be, although several supporting actors and the
        Beatles themselves are fine.

33 ANON. "Yeah? Yeah. Yeah!" Time, 84 (14 August), 67.
       Although made for exploitation, A Hard Day's Night is
    fresh and the Beatles are engaging; as a film about the
    Beatles it is inferior to the Maysles brothers' What's
    Happening.

34 ANON. "Yeah Indeed." Newsweek, 64 (24 August), 79.
       The New Wave approach makes A Hard Day's Night "fresh,
    lively." The "sardonic edge" makes it "surprisingly palat-
    able."

35 BAKER, PETER G. "A Hard Day's Night." Films and Filming, 10
    (August), 26.
       Notice says that the film "doesn't advance the technique
    of filmmaking," although it vitally brings across the
    Beatles' personalities and music.

*36 BEAN, ROBIN. "Keeping Up with the Beatles." Films and Film-
    ing, 10 (February), 9-12.

*37 BENAYOUN, ROBERT. "A Hard Day's Night." Positif, No. 66.
    [Cited in Eyquem, no. 446.]

38 BURKE, JOHN. A Hard Day's Night. New York: Dell Publishing,
    156 pp.
       Novelization of the film, with 8 pp. of stills.

39 COLEMAN, JOHN. Review of A Hard Day's Night. New Statesman,
    68 (10 July), 62.
       Film is "splendidly engaging"; several scenes are very
    funny. Much of the humor is in John Lennon's style, which
    is itself similar to the Marx Brothers'.

40 CROWTHER, BOSLEY. "A Hard Day's Night." New York Times
    (12 August), p. 41.
       Film is surprisingly good--like Marx Brothers comedy with
    "dazzling" camera style. Film seems "spontaneous," and the
    field romp "approaches audio-visual poetry."

41 DENT, ALAN. "Long Day's Hard Journey." Illustrated London
    News, 245 (18 July), 102.
       The Beatles have little talent, but some charm, little
    of which is revealed by A Hard Day's Night. The field romp
    is the one genuinely amusing scene.

42 FITZGIBBON, CONSTANTINE. "Beatle Film to Restore the Empire."
    Life, 57 (7 August), 15.

1964

        Discusses the Beatles phenomenon, concluding that A Hard Day's Night proves their fans right about their charm. The film defies pop-music conventions while dealing with the group's isolated existence.

43   GELDZAHLER, HENRY. "Fast, Energetic, and Hip." Vogue, 144 (15 September), 76.
        A Hard Day's Night's direction is knowing, the pace "lively," the film itself for the under-20 set.

44   HAGEN, RAY. "A Hard Day's Night." Films in Review, 15 (October), 503-505.
        Film is a "rush job," but at the same time "brisk, sharp, witty and wacky." The direction, editing, and the Beatles themselves as personalities make the film succeed.

45   HARTUNG, PHILIP T. "End of Summer." Commonweal, 80 (18 September), 638.
        Short review finds A Hard Day's Night irreverent, unpretentious, and "nicely filmed," with touches of surrealism. Sequences in cinéma vérité mode seem "amateurish and shaky."

46   KNIGHT, ARTHUR. "Beatles, Anyone?" Saturday Review, 47 (19 September), 30.
        The Beatles mystique is puzzling, but A Hard Day's Night shows them to be natural comedians. Film is almost good enough to be taken for a French New Wave work; its origins in that trend are obvious.

47   MALLETT, RICHARD. Review of A Hard Day's Night. Punch, 247 (22 July), 135.
        The balance of Pinteresque dialog and Chaplinesque visual humor is "skilful." The songs are integrated rather than imposed. The personalities and natural talents of the Beatles help make the movie an "all-round success."

48   NOWELL-SMITH, GEOFFREY. "A Hard Day's Night." Sight and Sound, 33 (Autumn), 196-97.
        The Beatles individually are unexceptional as are separate parts of the film; as a whole, however, it works, because of, rather than in spite of, its "slapdash" quality. Here, "B-picture badness" and "pure gold" mix precariously. The greatest failure is the TV studio sequence, which is too "distancing."

49   QUIGLY, ISABEL. "The Beatles: A Hard Day's Night." Spectator, 214 (10 July), 47.

1965

Film confirms all the discussion of the Beatles' charm.
Slim plot is fleshed out in treatment of their claustrophobic lifestyle.

50   RICH. "A Hard Day's Night." Variety, 235 (15 July), 6.
Beatles show great comedic promise, aided by the "brisk"
editing of John Jympson, the "spiky, funny, offbeat" script
of Alun Owen, the "vitality and inventiveness" of Lester's
direction, and a fine supporting cast.

51   STUART, WALKER. "A Slapstick Renaissance." Reporter, 31
(5 November), 42, 44.
A Hard Day's Night fits the Beatles' natural talents and
plays down their shortcomings by letting them interact
rather than act. The inspired camera work complements the
action and the songs are interpolated painlessly.

52   SUTHERLAND, ELIZABETH. "A Vote for the Sweet Parade." New
Republic, 151 (10 October), 26, 28.
A Hard Day's Night's success is due to its "integrity"
as it focuses on the group without imposing unnecessary
artificialities.

53   WEBB, PETER. "The Beatles Hit the Screen! Fresh Filmic Feat."
Christian Science Monitor [Eastern edition], 56 (3 August),
7.
A Hard Day's Night is humorous, poetic, surreal, the
directing and editing imaginative, but most of the credit
goes to the Beatles and their naturalness.

1965

54   ALPERT, HOLLIS. Review of Help! Saturday Review, 48 (28
August), 28.
Film is not up to its predecessor's standards--the Abbott
and Costello in Help! compared to the Marx Brothers' style
in A Hard Day's Night.

55   _____. "The Wilder Shores of Humor." Saturday Review, 48
(17 July), 24-25.
The Knack's "delights" have little to do with its plot
and much to do with the inventiveness of its visual humor.
It has meaning as a study of people asserting their individuality and "attempting wittily, madly, desperately" to
escape "mass absurdity."

1965

56   ANON. "Chase and Superchase." Time, 86 (3 September), 84.
In Help! the spontaneity of A Hard Day's Night is replaced by "highly professional, carefully calculated camera work and cutting" and some rapid-fire color footage.

57   ANON. "Help!" Avant-Scène du Cinéma, No. 53 (November), pp. 51-52.
Picture preview, French captions.

58   ANON. "The Knack." Films and Filming, 11 (July), 15-16.
Photo preview.

59   ANON. "New Breed." Newsweek, 66 (5 July), 82.
The Knack "swells with joy," abounds in camera tricks and talent. Short piece on Lester and his style.

60   ANON. "On the Scene." Playboy, 12 (October), 168-69.
Short profile of Lester.

61   ANON. "One Good Way to Film a Play." The Times [London] (3 June), p. 17.
Lester and writer Wood have "gaily and wisely" omitted all but the bare bones of the play version of The Knack, providing "glittering, extravagant variations."

62   ANON. Review of Help! Playboy, 12 (October), 26.
Film is funny although sometimes forced.

63   ANON. Review of The Knack. Playboy, 12 (August), 24.
"Knockout" film makes old plot line seem new. Direction, camera work, ensemble acting are all superior.

64   ANON. "Richard Lester--More Bounce to the Reel." Vogue, 146 (15 September), 112-13.
Short personality profile.

65   ANON. "Some Sense of Strain in Beatles Film." The Times [London] (29 July), p. 14.
Help! seems "more careless and slapdash" than A Hard Day's Night and The Knack, which were carefully crafted to seem "careless, slapdash, and spontaneous"--thus it is less funny.

66   ANON. "Three Men and a Girl." Time, 86 (9 July), 98.
In The Knack, Lester's visual gags often come at the expense of characterization. The gimmickry becomes annoying, as does the thickness of British accents.

67   BOYD, MALCOLM. "Sex, Sculpture, Sadism." Christian Century, 82 (15 December), 1547-48.
The Knack is totally Lester's as he succeeds in portraying four individuals in conflict with a mass society. The film's breeziness extends to its open treatment of "sex... as an unself-conscious subject of delight as well as of mystery."

68   CARTHEW, ANTHONY. "The Knack of Being Richard Lester." New York Times Magazine (8 August), pp. 16-17, 51-53.
Superficial but laudatory personality profile, interview excerpts, and survey of Lester's career up to Help!

69   CHAPIN, LOUIS. "The Knack." Christian Science Monitor [Eastern edition], 57 (4 August), 4.
Film is "restless" and "tasteless," with its smart dialog and New Wave techniques.

70   COLEMAN, JOHN. "Advertisements for the Beatles." New Statesman, 70 (30 July), 162-63.
Help! contains too many "cavortings and poses"; Lester runs the risk of becoming overly slick, but the film is still funny and charming.

71   _____. "Getting the Knack." New Statesman, 69 (4 June), 890.
Account of the Cannes Festival at which The Knack won the Golden Palm; review which praises the camera work, the improvisational quality, and the prolific gags.

72   CROWTHER, BOSLEY. "Help!" New York Times (24 August), p. 25.
Film lacks whatever made A Hard Day's Night special, although there are some interesting camera tricks.

73   _____. "The Knack." New York Times (1 July), p. 42.
Film breezes along at breakneck speed, given impetus and charm by, respectively, the lightning camera work and the ensemble of actors.

74   DENT, ALAN. "I Capitulate to These Divagations." Illustrated London News, 247 (14 August), 38.
Their music remains deplorable, but in Help! the Beatles display charm and "zest and gusto" in the style of the Marx Brothers.

75   _____. Review of The Knack. Illustrated London News, 246 (19 June), 32.
Film is well done by cast, director, and cameraman, but doesn't really seem worth doing, or seeing at all.

1965

76 DURGNAT, RAYMOND. "The Knack." <u>Films and Filming</u>, 11 (July), 25.
    Film effectively suspends realism without going too far and blends sex-oriented humor with sight gags. However, the funniness undermines the play's potential emotional power.

77 FONTENIA, CESAR S. "Cannes 65: <u>The Knack</u> de Richard Lester." <u>Nuestro Cine</u>, No. 42, pp. 40-42.
    Review, in Spanish.

*78 FRENCH, PHILIP. "Richard Lester." <u>Movie</u>, No. 14 (Autumn), pp. 5-11.
    [Cited in <u>British Humanities Index 1965</u>, p. 237.]

79 GILL, BRENDAN. "Hit or Miss." <u>New Yorker</u>, 41 (28 August), 101-102.
    <u>Help!</u> sometimes strains for gags, but most of them work wonderfully well--despite the "wholly unnecessary complexity" of the plot.

80 HARCOURT, PETER. "Help!" <u>Sight and Sound</u>, 34 (Autumn), 199-200.
    Discusses the Beatles' charisma and Lester's "endless enterprise" in supplying fresh visual fantasy. Suggests that the two Beatles films reveal reluctance to show the group as anything more than androgynous innocents. Finds "sadness" in the "lack of trust in how the Beatles really are."

81 HARDWICK, ELIZABETH. "Noisy, Sexy Breeziness." <u>Vogue</u>, 146 (15 August), 52.
    Short review; <u>The Knack</u> is a little less brilliant than <u>A Hard Day's Night</u>, with a few slow spots and some slightly inappropriate casting.

82 HARTUNG, PHILIP T. "A Comic Knack." <u>Commonweal</u>, 82 (2 July), 473.
    <u>The Knack</u> is as funny in its way as the great screwball comedies of the thirties and forties. Praise goes to Lester's expert direction.

83 HATCH, ROBERT. "The Knack." <u>Nation</u>, 201 (2 August), 68.
    Camera work and actors are most spirited elements in an essentially unexceptional story.

84 HEBEKER, KLAUS. "Richard Lester's <u>The Knack</u>." Film, No. 7 (July), pp. 10-13.
    Review, in German.

85   HINE, AL. Help! New York: Dell Publishing, 156 pp.
        Novelization of the screenplay with eight pages of
        stills.

86   HOBSON, HAROLD. "Help! The Beatles Take to Their Heels."
        Christian Science Monitor [Eastern edition], 57 (2 August),
        4.
        Review.

87   KAUFFMANN, STANLEY. "Beatles and Their Colleagues." New
        Republic, 153 (25 September), 34-35.
        The main problem with Help! lies in its easy comparison
        to A Hard Day's Night. The emphasis on plot makes Help! a
        somewhat different kind of film from the first, but it suc-
        ceeds largely due to Lester's cinematic sensitivity.

88   _____. "More Than a Knack." New Republic, 153 (10 July),
        29-30.
        Compares film The Knack with play; the film is inventive
        and exuberant at the expense of story and structure. Les-
        ter misses some important dramatic points, but his jokes
        are irresistible. He is one of the new generation of film-
        makers whose ideas are purely filmic, rather than something
        else, translated into film.

89   KENNEY, ANN D. "The Knack." Parents' Magazine, 40 (August),
        19.
        Short notice says plot is "slight and immoral" with
        "hilariously inventive" gags. Film lags a little, but
        nearly works.

90   LEFÈVRE, RAYMOND. "Le Knack et Comment l'Avoir." Cinéma,
        No. 99 (September/October), pp. 106-108.
        Lyrical essay about The Knack, in French.

*91 LEGRAND, GERARD. "The Knack." Positif, No. 71.
        [Cited in Eyquem, no. 446.]

92   LUDDY, TOM. Review of Help! Berkeley Barb, 1 (20 August), 3.
        The direction is a bit "over-wrought and self-indulgent,"
        and the plot is "intrusive." "Lester is still dishing up
        soufflés, still settling for pastiche when he could do much
        better," as in The Knack.

93   MACDONALD, DWIGHT. "The Knack." Esquire, 64 (October), 36,
        38.
        Film is "brilliant," "original," but not funny. It
        seems "overdirected," the slim play buried by the movie's
        tricks.

1965

94 MALLETT, RICHARD. Review of Help! Punch, 249 (4 August), 175.
    Plot is inconsequential, humor lively, and visuals extra-
    ordinary, particularly in the treatment of musical numbers.

95 _____. Review of The Knack. Punch, 248 (16 June), 900.
    Technically "dazzling" film manages to combine mature,
    "amoral" subject matter with contemporary dialog and slap-
    stick, and the result is inoffensive.

96 MILLER, EDWIN. "On the Scene with the Beatles." Seventeen,
    24 (August), 230-31, 280, 282, 284.
    General interview with the Beatles, asides by Lester and
    Shenson, producer of Help!, and stills from film.

97 MILNE, TOM. "The Knack." [BFI] Monthly Film Bulletin, 32
    (June), 88.
    Credits, synopsis, review which calls film half-awful,
    half-excellent. The alteration of the story from the stage
    play loses a good deal of playwright Jellicoe's insight,
    but several scenes show Lester's "fresh and sensitive"
    style.

98 OLIVER, EDITH. "Variations on a Theme by Jellicoe." New York-
    er, 41 (10 July), 54.
    Although not as perfect as A Hard Day's Night, The Knack
    is a visual poem with "sweetness and feeling" along with
    its high spirits.

99 PANTER-DOWNES, MOLLIE. "Letter from London." New Yorker, 41
    (26 June), 82, 84.
    The Knack is "wacky, original and hilarious," with spe-
    cial honors to David Watkin's brilliant cinematography.

100 PHILLIPE, PIERRE. "Au Secours!" Cinéma, No. 100 (November),
    pp. 128-29.
    In Help!, the Beatles are too passive to be given the
    title of "the new Marx Bros."

101 RICH. "Help!" Variety, 239 (4 August), 7.
    Camera work is a "delight"; in some sequences the film
    lags and Lester overindulges himself.

102 RIDER, DAVID. "Help!" Films and Filming, 12 (October), 27.
    Use of color is unfortunate—it slows up the comedy and
    makes the quick cuts and other camera tricks "hard on the
    eyes." The characters Foot and Algernon are unnecessary.

103 RONAN, MARGARET. "Help!" Senior Scholastic, 87 (30 September), 52.
     Film is "fantastic, frantic, punny and funny."

104 RUSSELL, FRANCIS. "Confessions of a Film Reviewer." National Review, 17 (5 October), 886, 888.
     The Knack is a "poor joke," comparable to home movies with adolescent camera tricks.

105 S., E. "Help!" [BFI] Monthly Film Bulletin, 32 (September), 133.
     Credits, synopsis, review which praises Lester's wit and visual sense, and points out how commercials have influenced his style.

106 SEELYE, JOHN. "Help!" Film Quarterly, 19 (Fall), 57-58.
     Amusing film is not, fortunately, an attempt to duplicate A Hard Day's Night; its lack of sharpness and its half-hearted satire make it inferior to the first film.

107 TATE, LAURENCE. "A Hard Day's Night: The Play's the Thing."
     The Paper [East Lansing, Michigan], 1 (10 December), 4.
     Film is "almost all joy," the Beatles at play, far superior to both "sadly decadent" later films, Help! and The Knack.

108 TAYLOR, JOHN RUSSELL. "The Knack." Sight and Sound, 34 (Summer), 148.
     With New Wave techniques firmly entrenched, gratuitously, in British cinema, the film is a pleasant surprise because its style evolves naturally. Although it isn't strictly "the film of the play," it has its own "coherence, logic and style."

109 UDOFF, YALE M. "The Knack." Film Quarterly, 19 (Fall), 55-57.
     Direction, cinematography, editing and score combine organically to give film vitality and inventiveness. Lester finds an unexpectedly lively London for his scenes, and succeeds in making his carefully structured film look spontaneous.

110 WALSH, MOIRA. "The Knack." America, 113 (24 July), 103.
     Lester's style gives the film its substance. Although sexually outspoken, the film poses no real moral problem, being satirical and "non-erotic." It is too gimmicky to be really great, but it is "a very funny and occasionally touching examination" of today's restless youth.

1965

111 WEALES, GERALD. "The Knack...and How to Lose It." Reporter,
     33 (23 September), 64.
         Compares film with play. Story becomes lost and "nihil-
     istic" when the one-room set is opened out and the Lester
     type of visual humor injected.

112 WENDT, ERNST. "Julia und die Beatles." Film, No. 12 (Decem-
     ber), pp. 10-15.
         Help! is discussed extensively in comparison with Juliet
     of the Spirits, in German.

113 _____. "The Knack und die Möglichkeiten der Groteske [The
     Knack and the Possibilities of the Grotesque]." Film,
     No. 9 (September), pp. 24-27.
         Analysis of The Knack, in German.

114 WHARTON, FLAVIA. "Help!" Films in Review, 16 (October), 513.
         Lester's directorial flair is omnipresent in the film
     but "beginning to show its limitations." The editing is
     "beyond praise."

115 _____. "The Knack." Films in Review, 16 (August/September),
     450.
         Notice seems to take the position that the resurgence
     of British physical comedy is a sort of gay in-joke.

116 ZATLYN, EDWARD. "Are You Ready?" Los Angeles Free Press, 2
     (30 July), 7.
         The Knack is the return of slapstick and old-time comedy.
     It is a poem about youth and love, a satire of sexual mores,
     the generation gap, and film itself. The editing is excel-
     lent, and the story's lesson--how to achieve emotional
     freedom--is well-expressed.

                              1966

117 ALPERT, HOLLIS. "New Faces--III." Saturday Review, 49 (24
     December), 21.
         Short biography and career piece on Lester.

118 _____. Review of A Funny Thing Happened on the Way to the
     Forum. Saturday Review, 49 (15 October), 26.
         Farce loses in the transition from play to film; perhaps
     Lester was allowed too much freedom. He loses its timing
     in making the comedy "cinematic," as in the "idiotic"
     chariot chase.

119   ANON. "Erotic Errors." Time, 88 (28 October), 111.
        Lester's "camerantics" confuse A Funny Thing Happened on
     the Way to the Forum; his style conflicts with Mostel's.

120   ANON. "A Funny Thing Happened on the Way to the Forum."
     Films and Filming, 13 (December), 10-11.
        Photo preview.

121   ANON. "Le Knack...et Comment l'Avoir." Avant-Scène du Cinéma,
     No. 59 (May), pp. 67-70.
        Synopsis, production notes, credits, digest of popular
     press comments, picture layout on The Knack, in French.

122   ANON. Review of A Funny Thing Happened on the Way to the
     Forum. Playboy, 13 (December), 48.
        Film is marred only by the drawn-out chariot race.

*123 BENAYOUN, ROBERT. "Visitez le Lestershire." Positif, No. 73.
        Concerns The Knack and Help! [Cited in Eyquem, no. 446.]

124   BLUESTONE, GEORGE [and RICHARD LESTER]. "Lunch With Lester."
     Film Quarterly, 19 (Summer), 12-16.
        Interview deals with Lester's early career, his general
     techniques and those used for certain effects in the Beatles
     films and others, and his future plans.

125   CANBY, VINCENT. "A Funny Thing Happened on the Way to the
     Forum." New York Times (17 October), p. 48.
        Lester has gone either too far or not far enough with
     his adaptation; his style is sometimes at odds with the
     material. Scenery, gags, and actors are all fine.

*126 COHN, BERNARD. "A Funny Thing Happened on the Way to the
     Forum." Positif, No. 90.
        [Cited in Eyquem, no. 446.]

127   ENNIS, PAUL. "A Funny Thing Happened on the Way to the Forum."
     Take One, 1 (February), 22.
        Most reviewers miss the point of why the film fails
     while play succeeds--film burlesque and stage burlesque have
     little in common. Thus, Lester's fault is less with his
     style than in the fact that "he was simply trying to reach
     the moon with a Zeppelin."

128   FEIFFER, JULES. "A Manic Montage of Raucous Rome." Life, 61
     (11 November), 10, 16.
        The gags, vaudeville and bawdy humor of A Funny Thing
     Happened on the Way to the Forum "congeal magically into

1966

art." It is "the best comedy...since A Hard Day's Night."
The play was never unified, but the screenplay becomes so
with Lester's touch. Concludes with a short discussion of
the changing nature of screen comedy.

129   GILL, BRENDAN. Review of A Funny Thing Happened on the Way to
the Forum. New Yorker, 42 (22 October), 164-65.
Film is funny although Lester's camera tricks ("in many
instances they are only tricks") are becoming overfamiliar.

130   GROSS, LEONARD. "John Lennon: Beatle on His Own." Look, 30
(13 December), 58-60, 62, 66.
Profile of, photos of, and interview with Lennon; inter-
spersed with descriptions of occurrences on the set of How
I Won the War and incidental profile of Lester.

131   HARTUNG, PHILIP T. "Three Comedies." Commonweal, 85 (28
October), 104, 106.
The script of A Funny Thing Happened on the Way to the
Forum is "clever," the cast "outstanding," and the direction
"freewheeling." Film is an amusing pastiche of operetta,
musical and Roman comedy.

132   KAEL, PAULINE. Review of A Funny Thing Happened on the Way to
the Forum. New Republic, 155 (10 December), 36-37.
Lester's cutting is "choppy" and thereby frustrating.
"The [viewing] experience becomes...like coitus interruptus
going on forever."

133   MACDONALD, DWIGHT. "Help!" Esquire, 65 (June), 52, 54.
Lester may be a has-been after three films. Help! is
like 92 minutes of commercials; it "strangles" the Beatles
in plot and "smothers" them in feathers. In areas of plot,
humor, and pace, A Hard Day's Night is the superior film.

134   MAXWELL, JAMES A. "Not So Funny." Reporter, 35 (29 December),
39.
Lester has "the power to convert stage gold into movie
lead," as evidenced by The Knack and A Funny Thing Happened
on the Way to the Forum. The latter's major faults are
draggy timing and the broad, theatrical performances of
some of the actors.

135   RINO. "A Funny Thing Happened on the Way to the Forum."
Variety, 244 (28 September), 6.
"Zesty scripting, imaginative directing and expert
clowning" combine the best of film musical comedy with a
Roman Empire epic take-off. The cast, particularly Mostel

and Gilford, is first-rate. Lester has finally molded sight gags into a "cohesive and structured whole."

136 SCHLESINGER, ARTHUR, JR. "Excellent Rowdy Fun." Vogue, 148 (December), 166.
     Lester's direction of A Funny Thing Happened on the Way to the Forum is clever but edgy and a bit forced. The camera tricks intrude, the chase scene is out of place, and the realism and intimacy undercut the comedy.

137 SMITH, LILY N. L. "A Funny Thing Happened on the Way to the Forum." Films in Review, 17 (November), 589-90.
     Movie is enjoyable, photography "lovely," cast hilarious.

138 SUGG, ALFRED R. "The Beatles and Film Art." Film Heritage, 1 (Summer), 3-13.
     Very complex scholarly article compares A Hard Day's Night and Help! with literature (particularly J. D. Salinger) and with each other, while remarking on general contrasts between film/literature and fact/fiction.

139 WALSH, MOIRA. "A Funny Thing Happened on the Way to the Forum." America, 115 (29 October), 526.
     Film makes fun of "Terence and Plautus and human cussedness in about equal proportions" as well as "itself and the New Wave." Lester's camera is "agile" and his sense of humor keeps the bawdy jokes on the right side of smuttiness.

140 WHITEHORN, ETHEL. "A Funny Thing Happened on the Way to the Forum." PTA Magazine, 61 (December), 38-39.
     Short notice calls film "generous and very funny entertainment."

1967

141 ANON. [and RICHARD LESTER]. "Richard Lester." New Yorker, 43 (28 October), 50-51.
     Profile and interview, dealing mainly with Lester's techniques, particularly his reasons for and methods of filming How I Won the War.

142 ANON. "Vaudeville of the Absurd." Time, 90 (17 November), 105.
     Satire in How I Won the War is undercut by use of the "just" WWII and by too many gratuitous gags, but is saved by its "dazzlingly surrealistic approach" and its frequent hilarity. Review is followed by a short piece on Lester.

1967

143   BILLINGTON, MICHAEL. "Film That Tilts at War Films." The
        Times [London] (18 October), p. 8.
           In How I Won the War, Lester's style works against the
        narrative, although he scores some direct hits against war
        films. Film might have been more effective if its charac-
        ters took the farce seriously.

144   BRAUCOURT, GUY. "Le Forum en Folie." Cinéma, No. 120 (Novem-
        ber), p. 127.
           The story of A Funny Thing Happened on the Way to the
        Forum is "stupid and vulgar." Lester, "brilliant" with the
        Beatles films and The Knack, directs this one ponderously.
        In French.

145   BRITT, GWENNETH. "How I Won the War." Films in Review, 18
        (November), 579-80.
           Short, violent notice calls film the product of possibly
        degenerate, probably traitorous "mod-monsters" incapable of
        rationality.

146   CASTELL, DAVID. "Styles in Collision." Illustrated London
        News, 250 (4 February), 32.
           Lester is one of the directors who, "having carved a
        niche, work themselves so deeply into it that it becomes a
        rut." In A Funny Thing Happened on the Way to the Forum,
        he imposes his style "without justification, reference or
        reverence" on the play and on the actors, whose styles are
        at variance with his.

147   COLEMAN, JOHN. "Lesterised." New Statesman, 73 (3 February),
        164.
           A Funny Thing Happened on the Way to the Forum is unex-
        pectedly spellbinding, using the medium "for all it's
        worth." Absurdist practices are best "when harnessed in
        art to comedy," and the quick-cut style is less self-con-
        scious in this film than in serious films "oppressed with
        messages."

148   _____. Review of How I Won the War. New Statesman, 74 (20
        October), 517.
           Most of film is "magnificently funny nonsense." Lester
        somewhat heavy-handedly assumes that his audience is nos-
        talgic about war's glamor.

149   CORLISS, RICHARD. Review of A Funny Thing Happened on the
        Way to the Forum. National Review, 19 (7 February), 153.
           Film's pace varies; it is easy to miss some jokes, but
        it is also easy to become bored, as during the chase.

Still, at least half of its 568 or 574 jokes work, which qualifies it as a funny film.

150 CROWTHER, BOSLEY. "How I Won the War." New York Times (9 November), p. 56.
Film's flaw is that war isn't funny. Some parts are amusing but the movie's ultimate effect is to make the audience feel "kicked in the teeth."

151 DAWSON, JAN. "How I Won the War." [BFI] Monthly Film Bulletin, 34 (November), 168-69.
Credits, synopsis, review which calls film brilliant in theory, but too detached. Lester's "gimmickry...does him a real disservice."

152 DENT, ALAN. "A Masterpiece--and Three Messes." Illustrated London News, 252 (4 November), 35.
Short review of How I Won the War finds its juxtaposition of farce and documentary senseless.

153 G., F. H. "A Funny Thing Happened...." Christian Science Monitor [Eastern edition], 59 (9 January), 6.
Cinematic style may disconcert fans of the stage version. Mostel, the mainstay of the play, is not given a chance to give a sustained performance.

154 GILL, BRENDAN. "I Laugh, Therefore I Am." New Yorker, 43 (18 November), 137.
Lester's anger is heavily felt in How I Won the War, which is a blanket, brutal indictment against all wars. It somehow forces us to laugh against our wishes and inclinations.

155 GILMAN, RICHARD. "Shooting Them Up." New Republic, 157 (25 November), 32-35.
How I Won the War is potentially more important for its influence on style than for its substance. Lester mocks notable war films to prevent his own from becoming one of them. He also distances the view by keeping the actors from becoming dramatis personae with comfortable stereotypes and by intermingling real and imitation newsreel footage, thus changing "our perception of art and history." The film's shortcomings include "occasional glibness" and "incomplete emotional commitment to its materials."

156 GOW, GORDON. "A Funny Thing Happened on the Way to the Forum." Films and Filming, 13 (April), 8.

1967

> Film retains humor of the play and expands some of the
> action well. Lester's camera effects become "too persis-
> tent," but he packs film with "inventiveness and enthusi-
> asm."

157   HANSON, CURTIS LEE [and RAY WAGNER]. "Two for the Show."
        Cinema, 3 (Winter), 4-8, 33.
        Conversation with Lester's co-producer dealing with
        problems encountered while producing Petulia.

158   HAROLDSON, THOMAS. "How I Won the War--'Brilliant.'" Fifth
        Estate [Detroit], 2 (15 December), 17.
        Film is "one of the most active and complicated" ever
        made. It is rich with multi-leveled meanings and "subver-
        sive" techniques, the most insidious of which is the manipu-
        lation of our feelings for Sgt. Transom. He is the only
        "real" character, a "good soldier" with whom it is only too
        easy to identify, although he is the embodiment of what the
        film opposes.

159   HARTUNG, PHILIP T. "No Flag, No Rally." Commonweal, 87 (15
        December), 359-60.
        How I Won the War is episodic and alienating. Lester's
        intent is laudable, but his approach is "scattered" and
        lacks discipline.

160   HATCH, ROBERT. Review of How I Won the War. Nation, 205
        (13 November), 506, 508.
        Film contains "maximum energy and minimum efficiency,"
        directing its "nihilism" against itself. Flaws are length,
        redundancy, strain, and that "its principal complaint seems
        to be that soldiers, and particularly officers, are shock-
        ing bad craftsmen."

161   HOUSTON, PENELOPE. "How I Won the War." Sight and Sound, 36
        (Autumn), 202.
        The intent to jolt the audience is undermined by the
        fragmented style. The film's simple message is lost
        through "technical indirection."

162   KLEISS, WERNER. "Toll Trieben es die Alten Römer [Old Rome
        Gone Mad]." Film, 5 (May), 34.
        Review of A Funny Thing Happened on the Way to the Forum,
        in German.

163   _____. "Wie Ich den Krieg Gewann [How I Won the War]." Film,
        5 (December), 26.
        Review, in German.

164   KNIGHT, ARTHUR. Review of How I Won the War. Saturday Review,
      50 (18 November), 57.
          Notice calls film a well-intended muddle in its attempt
      to be both anti-war and anti-war-film.

165   KOZLOFF, MAX, WILLIAM JOHNSON, and RICHARD CORLISS. "Shooting
      at Wars: Three Views." Film Quarterly, 21 (Winter 1967/
      68), 27-36.
          Kozloff discusses The Battle of Algiers and Far from
      Vietnam. Johnson discusses the latter and How I Won the
      War, whose most effective device is the "alternation of
      humor and horror" which provides shock contrasts and keeps
      the viewer's outrage directed at what Lester is portraying
      rather than at himself and his "sick humor." He has, how-
      ever, chosen to adapt not an anti-war book, but one which
      is against inefficiency in warfare. The film's attitudes
      are confused by this and other flaws. Corliss discusses
      How I Won the War. Although Lester has avoided comment on
      Vietnam, he has gone further than any other commercial di-
      rector with his anti-war stance. Film is flawed by its
      double targets, war and war films. Critics who complained
      that the film isn't funny missed its point; it is supposed
      to, and does, elicit a response of horror.

166   KRANTZ, LEIF. "Hur Jag Vann Kriget [How I Won the War]."
      Chaplin, No. 77, p. 345.
          Review, in Swedish.

167   MALLETT, RICHARD. Review of A Funny Thing Happened on the Way
      to the Forum. Punch, 252 (8 February), 206-207.
          Film is "often funny" although it tries too hard to be
      so. Mostel is the main force behind its success.

168   _____. Review of How I Won the War. Punch, 253 (25 October),
      633.
          Film has many good moments, despite laughter-killing
      shock footage.

169   MORGENSTERN, JOSEPH. "A Hard Day's War." Newsweek, 70 (20
      November), 106.
          How I Won the War contains some hilarious bits of satire,
      but many more which don't work because "the director...can-
      not keep track of himself or his targets."

170   MURF. "How I Won the War." Variety, 248 (25 October), 6.
          Film is forced, "substitutes motion for emotion, reeling
      for feeling, and crude slapstick for telling satire."

1967

171   RICHARDSON, BOYCE [and RICHARD LESTER]. "Dick Lester and His
         War." Take One, 1 (December), 4-6.
            Interview discusses How I Won the War, briefly summarizes
         Lester's career, deals with film technique (Lester professes
         suspicion of technical tricks), the philosophy behind his
         new Petulia, and his moral viewpoint.

172   RIPP, JUDITH. "How I Won the War." Parents' Magazine, 42
         (December), 27.
            Notice says that film doesn't completely succeed, but it
         is a "valiant effort."

173   SCHICKEL, RICHARD. "The Pop-Pop-Pop Film Is a Dud Against
         War." Life, 63 (17 November), 8.
            How I Won the War cancels its own message with its inep-
         titude; it alienates the audience from the emotions it
         should be experiencing. By making war surreal rather than
         real, Lester trivializes it.

174   SCHLESINGER, ARTHUR, JR. "Brilliant, Unnerving." Vogue, 150
         (December), 175.
            How I Won the War is the best film of its kind since Dr.
         Strangelove; the script is deadly apt, the cutting bold,
         "the pressure incessant."

175   SHAPIRO, JERRY. Review of How I Won the War. News Project
         [Flushing, New York], 1 (7 December), 11.
            Lester tells us what we already know about war; his tone
         is that of a lecturer.

176   SHEED, WILFRID. Review of A Funny Thing Happened on the Way
         to the Forum. Esquire, 67 (March), 22.
            Lester manipulates actors rather than letting them act.
         This works for the play, but not for Mostel. The slapstick
         is "arbitrary," as is Lester's homage to "every last one"
         of the "pure cinematic" low comedy bits. He still does
         "indifferent things well and good things beautifully."

177   SWEENEY, LOUISE. "Lester's How I Won the War." Christian
         Science Monitor [Eastern edition], 59 (24 November), 14.
            Film functions as an anti-war film and an "anti-war-film
         film." Lester's satire isn't sharp or black enough, and in
         some ways his choice of WWII as his focus is not right.

178   TAYLOR, JOHN RUSSELL. "Film Falls Between Two Styles." The
         Times [London] (2 February), p. 5.
            A Funny Thing Happened on the Way to the Forum is ami-
         able, but disappointing in light of Lester's earlier films.

His style is at variance with the actors', the quick cut
versus the slow burn.

179 _____. "A Funny Thing Happened on the Way to the Forum."
[BFI] Monthly Film Bulletin, 34 (February), 41.
Credits, synopsis, review which complains that many of
the comics' jokes are clipped short by the pace, and that
there seems to be "an apparent lack of sympathy between the
director and his material." He makes more of the "diverting
scribbles round the edges" than he does of the main plot.

180 WALSH, MOIRA. "How I Won the War." America, 117 (25 November), 668.
Film is "poor and silly." Lester seems to think his
audience can't perceive anything it hasn't been bludgeoned
with, an ultimately self-defeating point of view.

181 WHITEHALL, RICHARD. "Disturbing Film." Open City [Los Ange-
les], No. 29 (10 November), p. 9.
Lester's mix of slapstick and alienation in How I Won
the War is "brilliantly" successful. Some of the same effects that were "window dressing" in previous films are
totally integrated in this one.

1968

182 ADLER, RENATA. Review of Petulia. New York Times (11 June),
p. 54.
The "strange, lovely, nervous little film" contains frag-
ments of narrative which economically reveal characters and
situations. Lester successfully uses his comedy-film
techniques in this serious film.

183 ANON. "How I Won the War." The American Dream [Tempe, Ari-
zona], 1:11.
Film is the year's best and most daring, challenging as
it does the justness of even the near-sacred Second World
War.

184 ANON. "How I Won the War." Filmfacts, 10 (1 January), 360-62.
Credits, synopsis, digest of popular press reviews.

185 ANON. "How I Won the War." Good Morning Teaspoon [San Fran-
cisco], 4 (1 May), 6.
Review.

1968

186   ANON. "Lester." <u>Logos</u> [Montreal], 1 (March?), 13.
      In <u>How I Won the War</u>, Lester "psychs out" the audience,
      first playing up to its expectations, then reversing them.

187   ANON. "Petulia." <u>Filmfacts</u>, 11 (1 July), 159-61.
      Credits, synopsis, digest of popular press reviews.

188   ANON. "Petulia." <u>Films and Filming</u>, 14 (August), 34-35.
      Photo preview.

189   ANON. Review of <u>How I Won the War</u>. <u>Playboy</u>, 15 (January), 38.
      A near-great film is needed to "strike out at war"--this
      one is not even good.

190   ANON. Review of <u>Petulia</u>. <u>Playboy</u>, 15 (June), 34.
      "Serious comedy" about people who use people has a "po-
      tent sense of truth."

191   ANON. Review of <u>Petulia</u>. <u>Time</u>, 91 (14 June), 91.
      The actors have little to do, but Lester enjoys himself
      satirizing San Francisco and contemporary society.

192   ANON. "Spröde Verpackung [Brittle Wrapping]." <u>Der Spiegel</u>,
      22 (11 November), 210.
      Review of <u>Petulia</u>, in German.

193   ARMSTRONG, MARION. "Guts and Grace." <u>Christian Century</u>, 85
      (4 September), 1110.
      Lester's direction of <u>Petulia</u> is "sensitive as well as
      sportively ironic." The film is "a celebration of integri-
      ty," particularly Petulia's.

194   ____. "Savage Satire." <u>Christian Century</u>, 85 (24 January),
      117-18.
      <u>How I Won the War</u> is suitable for viewing by those who
      wish to hate themselves and their world. Satire of this
      particular war in this particular way is not quite fair.

195   AUSTEN, DAVID. "Petulia." <u>Films and Filming</u>, 14 (September),
      33-34.
      The film is dense with "information"; it deals with "emo-
      tional aggression" rather than "romantic fulfillment." A
      flaw is that Petulia is too "calculating" to be a real kook.

*196 BENAYOUN, ROBERT. "Petulia." <u>Positif</u>, No. 102.
      [Cited in Eyquem, no. 446.]

197 BILLINGTON, MICHAEL. "Jazzing Up the Eternal Triangle." The
  Times [London] (13 June), p. 15.
    In Petulia, Lester's mannerisms are becoming obtrusive.
  They suited the Beatles films, but lately style has been at
  odds with content. In this film it obscures the plot, but
  the performances help to convey the story's pain.

198 _____. Review of Petulia. Illustrated London News, 252 (22
  June), 32.
    The film works despite Lester's jumpy style; he somehow
  manages to "intensify the feeling of pain" present in the
  book upon which it was based.

199 BIRSTEIN, ANN. "Petulia--Beautiful When She is Plain." Vogue,
  151 (June), 82.
    What was probably intended as a "brutal, sophisticated
  tragicomedy" ends up as a "nice, sentimental love story."
  Chemistry between the lead actors is lacking, but the performances are good and Lester's observations are witty.

200 BRAUCOURT, GUY. "Comment J'Ai Gagné la Guerre [How I Won the
  War]." Cinéma, No. 126 (May), pp. 103-106.
    Two aspects of How I Won the War are troublesome: the
  humor is too British to be fully enjoyed by a non-Britisher;
  the story's construction is "tortuous" because of the time-
  space distortions. In French.

201 C., P. "How I Won the War." Helix [Seattle], 3 (14 February?),
  8.
    Notice calls film "a technical pretension," which,
  through its lack of "style," voids the truths it tries to
  present.

202 CAMERON, IAN, MARK SHIVAS [and RICHARD LESTER]. "Interview
  with Richard Lester." Movie, No. 16 (Winter 1968/69),
  pp. 16-28.
    Probably Lester's best "pre-renaissance" interview, deal-
  ing thoroughly with his career up to The Bed-Sitting Room.

203 CHRISTGAU, ROBERT. "As Others See Us." Ramparts, 7 (24
  August), 54, 56.
    Petulia "both exhibits and embodies an emotionless
  state." The nervous style fits the content, but it isn't
  easy to watch. The satire "never comes off" because nothing
  is picked on, just set down by the camera.

204 CICARELLA, JAMES. "Close-Up: Petulia." Williamette Bridge
  [Portland, Oregon], 1 (16 August), 14.

1968

> Surprisingly, Lester's films have not become repetitive. *Petulia*, his "greatest challenge" to the audience, is a "poignant," beautifully filmed study of America.

*205   CIMENT, MICHEL. "How I Won the War." *Positif*, No. 95. [Cited in Eyquem, no. 446.]

206   COLEMAN, JOHN. "Poor Rich." *New Statesman*, 75 (21 June), 846-47.
> *Petulia* is Lester's "most vulnerable and best film to date"--his first real exploration of the human condition. His commercial training sometimes shows but is sometimes also an advantage. The performances are as important as his style.

207   CORLISS, RICHARD. Review of *Petulia*. *National Review*, 20 (24 September), 969-70.
> Lester usually makes his audience work at laughing, but he has relaxed his overkill method with *Petulia*, which is not a comedy. The style nearly dislocates the plot, but in doing so is "relevant and revelatory."

208   CRIST, JUDITH. Review of *Petulia*. *New York*, 1 (17 June), 45.
> Lester is "becoming a captive of his style" and is "exploiting it for its own sake." Julie Christie is miscast and Lester is too busy stylizing to worry about his story. George C. Scott's performance is the best thing about the film; others are fine.

209   DAWSON, JAN. "*Petulia*." [BFI] *Monthly Film Bulletin*, 35 (August), 113.
> Credits, synopsis, review which points out that the film's emphasis on the impossibility of developing human relationships in swinging society is undermined by the style, which "reaffirms the myth" of that society.

210   ELISCU, LITA. Review of *Petulia*. *East Village Other* [New York], 3 (12 July), 18.
> The film is about pain and the painful relationship of two people. Editing style enhances the total "discontinuous effect."

211   GILLIATT, PENELOPE. "Anguish Under the Skin." *New Yorker*, 44 (15 June), 87.
> *Petulia* concerns pain, and the way in which the central characters deal, or fail to deal, with it. Lester, always a "visibly brilliant director," has used his actors and techniques to make a "passionate" film. Its accuracy in

portraying contemporary insensitivity is "grieving and dis-
tinct."

212 GREENSPUN, ROGER. "Praise for Petulia." New York Free Press,
     1 (20 June), 7.
       Review.

213 HAMPE, BARRY. "An Evening of Fun at World War II." Distant
     Drummer [Philadelphia], 1:20.
       Lester has "no business" doing a theme film; the message
     of How I Won the War hampers his comedy and ultimately has
     little effect. Although not an "important" film, it has
     its share of funny, bizarre moments.

214 HAROLDSON, THOMAS. "Petulia at the Studio." Fifth Estate
     [Detroit], 3 (5 September), 17.
       In this "unimpressive" picture, the serious things are
     vaguely farcical, the farcical aren't funny, and the
     technique is "dated."

215 HARTUNG, PHILIP T. "Games Movies Play." Commonweal, 88 (28
     June), 443.
       Petulia is "difficult" and stylistically brilliant. The
     time distortions are hard to follow, but Lester's comments
     on "today's thoughtless society" are worth the trouble.
     The continuing theme is our lack of "concern for our fellow
     man"; it is Lester's best film since The Knack.

216 HATCH, ROBERT. Review of Petulia. Nation, 207 (8 July), 29.
       Film is about "how people...don't communicate with one
     another." It is a bit jaded because of the ephemeral
     quality of pop jargon and idiom. The film starts promising-
     ly but gets involved in so much "psychedelic flash and de-
     racinated editing" that nothing much follows through.

217 KAUFFMANN, STANLEY. "Lesser But Lester." New Republic, 158
     (29 June), 22, 33-34.
       Petulia's script is flawed, with odd gaps and emphases.
     Actors, save George C. Scott, are average to poor. It is
     Lester's "incessant imagination" which makes the film work
     at all. The TV-commercial techniques are particularly
     fitted to the Mod satire. In general, the use of the sub-
     liminal flash can be too literal, squelching the imagina-
     tions of both actors and audience. However, of the direc-
     tors using it in the "relatively new" way of "tracing out
     the lightning of the mind on film," Lester is one of the
     best.

1968

218   LLINAS, FRANCISCO. "Aproximación a Richard Lester [Meeting with Richard Lester]." <u>Nuestro Cine</u>, No. 72 (April), pp. 26-29.
     Discussion of <u>A Hard Day's Night</u>, <u>Help!</u>, <u>The Knack</u>, and <u>A Funny Thing Happened on the Way to the Forum</u>, with cast and technical credits for the latter, in Spanish.

219   McMAHAN, IDA and ETHEL WHITEHORN. "<u>How I Won the War</u>." <u>PTA Magazine</u>, 62 (January), 39.
     Notice calls film "confusing and disturbing."

220   MALLETT, RICHARD. Review of <u>Petulia</u>. <u>Punch</u>, 254 (19 June), 899.
     Lester's comedy techniques are "not quite successful," sometimes "distracting and detaching." Around the plot is a lot of "highly entertaining decoration," fascinating to look at.

221   MORGENSTERN, JOSEPH. "Total Put-Down." <u>Newsweek</u>, 71 (17 June), 90.
     <u>Petulia</u> is a "rotten, dishonest comedy" which leaves doubt whether Lester likes or hates his characters. The film is the work "of an opportunistic, deracinated entertainer who keeps up with the affairs of his homeland from London by going to see <u>The Loved One</u>."

222   MURF. "<u>Petulia</u>." <u>Variety</u>, 250 (1 May), 26.
     Film is an "intelligent, perceptive, and lucid blend of story and style." The audience's point of view will determine whether they see "compassion (not necessarily sympathy) for human foibles" or cynicism in the film.

223   PRICE, JAMES. "<u>Petulia</u>." <u>Sight and Sound</u>, 37 (Summer), 154-55.
     This is the first Lester film with "heart": the complex structure seems to be his way of overcoming his "embarassment" at approaching relationships. The result is richer than his usual product.

224   PROKOSCH, MIKE. "Richard Lester and <u>Petulia</u>." <u>Old Mole</u> [Cambridge, Massachusetts], 1 (13 September), 12.
     Discusses Lester's earlier films in terms of visual style, and <u>Petulia</u> as it relates to his work so far.

225   RIPP, JUDITH. "<u>Petulia</u>." <u>Parents' Magazine</u>, 43 (May), 34.
     Notice calls film an "interestingly tricked-out romance."

226   ROBINSON, BARRY. "<u>How I Won the War</u>." <u>Media and Methods</u>, 4 (January), 42-43.

1968

The film is not a comedy, but rather a black farce which uses comedy to "illuminate the agonies and follies of... war."

227 SCHICKEL, RICHARD. "A Savage Yelp from Affluencia." Life, 64 (31 May), 12.
Petulia has "ferocious and ultimately purifying energy," due to Lester's "passionate intensity" and the "highly charged style" with which he presents his materialistic vision. The film's style is "organically related" to its substance.

228 SHEED, WILFRID. Review of How I Won the War. Esquire, 69 (January), 29, 32.
Lester debunks the entertainment aspects of war--the war movie, the glory of war, etc., and does it well. He falters in using the British army, thus getting entangled in class-structure considerations and also leaving room for too many light-hearted English digressions.

229 _____. Review of Petulia. Esquire, 70 (October), 90, 92.
The film suffers from Lester's "slickness and shallow-ness" which are "built right into his method"; the time distortion obscures more than it reveals. Still, the film is interesting, and Lester has a good eye for the actors he uses.

230 SHEETS, KEVIN. "Les Fleurs d'Ennui." Spectator [Bloomington, Indiana], 7 (1 October), 8-9.
Petulia's characters are one-dimensional and lifeless. Film is "interesting...but not...excellent," because it has "limited the abilities of life-styles to be other than a clinically defined pattern of existence."

231 SHIVAS, MARK. "Nåja, Bomben Duger i Alla Fall att Skrattas Åt [Well, Anyway, the Bomb is Fit to Laugh At]." Chaplin, No. 85, pp. 296-97.
Discusses The Bed-Sitting Room and Petulia, in Swedish.

232 SONE, HAL L. "Anti-War Films in Spotlight." North Valley Free Press [Chico, California], 1 (7 February), 8.
Review of How I Won the War.

233 SWEENEY, LOUISE. "Petulia: Lester's Cinematic Assault on Empty Affluence." Christian Science Monitor [Eastern edi-tion], 60 (21 June), 6.
Review.

1968

234 TOUGAS, K. "Petulia." Georgia Straight [Vancouver, Canada],
     2 (23 August), 17.
          Short review likens style to Alain Resnais's; all the
     parts of the film combine into a "lively totality." Lester
     isn't a "vital creator," but an "accomplished entertainer."

235 TYNAN, KENNETH, RICHARD LESTER and CHARLES WOOD. "Lester:
     Mir Wird Schlect." Film, 6 (January).
          Tynan interviews Lester and screenwriter Wood about How
     I Won the War. In German.

236 WALKER, VALERIE L. "How I Won What?" Seed [Chicago], 2:16.
          How I Won the War is, in the opinion of a British Jew,
     "the World War II movie to end all World War II movies."

237 WENDT, ERNST. "Fuck for Peace (Make Films Not War)." Film,
     6 (January).
          Discussion, in German, of How I Won the War and Les
     Carabiniers.

238 WHITEHALL, RICHARD. "Putting Down Petulia." Open City [Los
     Angeles], No. 67 (30 August), p. 8.
          Lester's films all "hard-sell" something; this one, the
     shakiness of marriage. The pain of unstable relationships
     is turned "pretty" and trendy. Compared to a comparable
     film by Godard, Lester's is brittle; he exploits the inno-
     vations of others.

239 WHITEHORN, ETHEL. "Petulia." PTA Magazine, 63 (September),
     39.
          Notice observes film "swiftly and gracefully told."

240 YOUNGBLOOD, GENE. "Lester Wins the War by Default." Los
     Angeles Free Press, 5 (9 February), 12.
          Lester is an "adolescent, non-intellectual, non-philoso-
     phical quasi-artist" who ruins every good idea he has. He
     was the wrong man to make How I Won the War, which in his
     hands doesn't come on strong enough. Its major flaw is the
     Brechtian distancing.

1969

241 ANON. [and RICHARD LESTER]. "Londres: Encuentro con Richard
     Lester [London: Encounter with Richard Lester]." Nuestro
     Cine, No. 83 (March), pp. 13-16.
          Interview, touching on How I Won the War in relation to
     The Bed-Sitting Room, the intricacies of film financing and
     distribution, etc. In Spanish.

242   CANBY, VINCENT. "The Bed-Sitting Room is at Little Carnegie."
      New York Times (29 September), p. 53.
           Lester's films "get worse in direct relation to the
      seriousness of their intentions." This one is over-absurd,
      giving holocaust the meaningfulness of "a well-aimed custard
      pie." Lester's direction is surprisingly subdued, although
      the film "could have used a few tricks."

243   CRIST, JUDITH. Review of The Bed-Sitting Room. New York, 2
      (20 October), 63.
           Notice calls film a "flatulent, snail-paced series of
      Goon Show discards."

244   GUBERN GARRIGA-NOGUÉS, ROMÁN. "Lester, Richard." In Enciclo-
      pedia Ilustrada del Cine. Volume 2. Barcelona: Editorial
      Labor, S. A., p. 293.
           Short, basic career article, emphasizing Lester's sur-
      real style, in Spanish.

245   HATCH, ROBERT. Review of The Bed-Sitting Room. Nation, 209
      (27 October), 452-53.
           The slag-heap sets are the best part of the film, whose
      overall effect is "coy." Lester "has been given an extreme
      situation without sufficient detail to animate it."

246   KAEL, PAULINE. Review of The Bed-Sitting Room. New Yorker,
      45 (11 October), 158-59.
           The film is similar to The Running, Jumping, and Stand-
      ing Still Film; its "chaos becomes numbing." It "lacks the
      simplicity of feeling" that makes other anti-war films ef-
      fective.

247   KAUFFMANN, STANLEY. Review of The Bed-Sitting Room. New
      Republic, 161 (18 October), 22, 32.
           How I Won the War is much stronger than this film, part-
      ly because it is revelatory, while this one has an odd
      script which Lester seems content to fumble along with.
      The two unassailable aspects of The Bed-Sitting Room are
      its photography and its acting.

248   KLEISS, WERNER. "Kein Schöner Blödsinn [No Beautiful Non-
      sense]." Film, 7 (August), 37-38.
           Review of The Bed-Sitting Room, in German.

249   MARTIN, JAMES. "How I Won the War." Open City [Los Angeles],
      2 (2 February), 14.
           The film is sometimes confusing and irritating, always
      exciting. Its humor is too British to be consistently

1969

> funny. Contrary to the Schickel review [No. 173], Lester
> isn't anti-war so much as he is against our remembrances of
> war as glorious.

250 MARTIN, MARCEL. "Petulia--Une Anti-Comedie Americaine." Ciné-
     ma, No. 135 (April), pp. 122-24.
> The film is "beautiful" and "important." It would be im-
> proper to criticize it for being confusing; the flashes back
> and forward are not a "vain coquetry," but a valid device
> for psychological revelation. Lester comments on America
> as Godard does on France.

251 MORGENSTERN, JOSEPH. "Bad Neighborhood." Newsweek, 74 (3
     November), 97-98.
> The Bed-Sitting Room is a "dim postwar farce" which is
> too "remote" to have an effect on the audience.

252 PRELUTSKY, BURT. "What's Richard Lester Trying to Do?" Holi-
     day, 45 (April), 82-83, 122-24.
> Jaundiced view of Lester's work up to Petulia; each film
> is derivative of the others. "It seems to be his aesthetic
> opinion that fast is somehow synonymous with funny." Quotes
> Stephen Sondheim's calling him a "second echelon director"
> who, with Petulia, is finally making his gimmicks work to
> illuminate character.

253 RIPP, JUDITH. "The Bed-Sitting Room." Parents' Magazine, 44
     (December), 12, 26.
> Notice.

1970

254 ANON. "Lester, Richard." In Current Biography 1969. Edited
     by Charles Moritz. New York: H. W. Wilson Company,
     pp. 253-55.
> Biography and concise career article which includes
> quotes representative of critical reactions to each film.

255 ANON. Review of The Bed-Sitting Room. Playboy, 17 (January),
     36.
> One in ten gag situations are "intrinsically funny," the
> rest seem "superimposed."

256 ANON. [and RICHARD LESTER]. "Richard Lester." In Directors
     at Work. Edited by Bernard R. Kantor, Irwin R. Blacker and
     Anne Kramer. New York: Funk and Wagnalls, pp. 223-63.

Discusses Lester's career from early days to <u>Petulia</u>; his methods of developing screenplays and of working; his philosophy; his views of society and of the function of a filmmaker; the films he likes to watch; his opinions on the "new talent" in film and on where film is going, etc.

257 CAMPBELL, RUSSELL. "The Bed-Sitting Room." [BFI] <u>Monthly Film Bulletin</u>, 37 (April), 67-68.
Credits, synopsis, review which says film fails due to its absence of a sense of time and plot. Done differently, it might have been a "devastating critique of 'civilised' society and its pathetic values."

258 COLEMAN, JOHN. Review of <u>The Bed-Sitting Room</u>. <u>New Statesman</u>, 79 (3 April), 484.
Although strange, the film has its moments.

259 GELMIS, JOSEPH [and RICHARD LESTER]. "Richard Lester." In his <u>The Film Director as Superstar</u>. Garden City, N. Y.: Doubleday and Company, Inc., pp. 231-63.
Some films and Lester's methods are discussed in considerable detail. Lester explains why he is more interested in his failures than in his successes: "Success is terribly ephemeral and failure is lasting."

260 HOUSTON, PENELOPE. Review of <u>The Bed-Sitting Room</u>. <u>Spectator</u>, 224 (4 April), 451.
Film suffers because of dated theme and the use of "incessant restlessness as a substitute for pace." It appears to be a solid filmmaker's idea gone wrong on the screen.

*261 LANGLEY, LEE. "Snap, Crackle, Boom!" <u>Guardian</u> [Manchester] (25 March), p. 10.
[Cited in <u>British Humanities Index 1970</u>, p. 237.]

262 MALLETT, RICHARD. Review of <u>The Bed-Sitting Room</u>. <u>Punch</u>, 258 (8 April), 540.
Film is disappointing due to the throwaway nature of some of the best jokes.

263 MILLER, GAVIN. "Oh, Calamity!" <u>Listener</u>, 83 (2 April), 463.
Lester keeps <u>The Bed-Sitting Room</u> moving along, with special help from production designer Assheton Gorton and the cast.

*264 PÉREZ, MICHEL. "The Bed-Sitting Room." <u>Positif</u>, No. 110.
[Cited in Eyquem, no. 446.]

1970

265 SCHRECK, STEPHEN. Review of How I Won the War. Prairie Fire
     [Regina, Canada], 1 (10 February), 6.
     Reprinted from Ramparts.

266 TARRATT, MARGARET. "The Bed-Sitting Room." Films and Filming,
     16 (May), 42.
     Film is a collection of individual performances lacking
     unity. Milligan's surreal play is unsuccessfully forced
     into a bomb-oriented black comedy.

1971

267 DEMPSEY, MICHAEL. "War as Movie Theater--Two Films." Film
     Quarterly, 25 (Winter), 33-36.
     The comedic approach to war failed in How I Won the War
     but succeeds in The Bed-Sitting Room. The stylization of
     the set helps the latter film succeed by creating a surreal
     environment for surreal circumstances. Lester avoids emo-
     tionalism in general, which gives his occasional "epiphanies"
     added poignance. The Bed-Sitting Room "extends the range of
     his expressiveness"; some of the "gaiety" of the earlier
     films comes through unexpectedly.

268 GOLDMAN, FREDERICK. "The Bed-Sitting Room." Film News, 28
     (June/July), 26.
     The film needs no scenes of horror--"the illogicality
     and absurdity of the commonplace is itself horrible." The
     dialog is brilliant; it makes demands of the audience.
     This, and the "success of the film's Golgotha ambience" may
     account for its box office failure when first released.

1972

269 CUTLER, BILL. "The Bed-Sitting Room." Great Speckled Bird
     [Atlanta], 5 (14 February), 12.
     Review.

270 HINXMAN, MARGARET. "Lester, Richard." In International En-
     cyclopedia of Film. Edited by Roger Manvell and Lewis
     Jacobs. New York: Crown Publishers, Inc., p. 338.
     Very short but intelligent summary of Lester's style.

271 ROSS, ARTHUR. "The Bed-Sitting Room." Los Angeles Free Press,
     9 (19 May), Part I, p. 14.
     In some of his earlier work, Lester's style is employed
     purposelessly. The Bed-Sitting Room is the "culmination"

of his career in which he forsakes much of his former style in order to satirize the state and the bourgeoisie.

272 SADOUL, GEORGES and PETER MORRIS. "Hard Day's Night (A)." In their Dictionary of Films. Berkeley and Los Angeles: University of California Press, pp. 145-46.
Very brief but concise discussion of Lester's style in the film.

273 _____. "Help!" In their Dictionary of Films. Berkeley and Los Angeles: University of California Press, p. 147.
Short, pithy critique of the film.

274 _____. "Lester, Richard." In their Dictionary of Film Makers. Berkeley and Los Angeles: University of California Press, p. 153.
Short, concise piece traces Lester's style development; he is fast and clever without being merely fashionable, and with Petulia "his work took on new depth and assurance."

275 _____. "Petulia." In their Dictionary of Films. Berkeley and Los Angeles: University of California Press, p. 282.
Short critique--"the fragmentary narrative technique... brilliantly reflects the swinging world and its disjointed relationships."

1973

276 ANON. "Lester, Richard." In Celebrity Register. Edited by Earl Blackwell. New York: Simon and Schuster, p. 290.
Short personality profile.

277 DELAIN, MICHEL, MICHEL CIMENT [and RICHARD LESTER]. "Dumas Revue par Lester." L'Express, No. 1170 (10 December), pp. 48-49.
Review of The Three Musketeers and a short, interesting interview with Lester, in French.

278 HALL, WILLIAM [and RICHARD LESTER]. "Richard Lester." In Directors in Action. Edited by Bob Thomas. Indianapolis and New York: Bobbs Merrill Co., Inc., pp. 72-75.
Interview deals with Lester's style and his work on commercials.

279 McBRIDE, JOSEPH [and RICHARD LESTER]. "Running, Jumping and Standing Still: an Interview with Richard Lester." Sight and Sound, 42 (Spring), 75-79.

1973

        Discusses The Three Musketeers, still in pre-planning
stages; his other films; the influence of Buster Keaton on
his style; his ideas about filmmaking.

280   MOSK. "The Three Musketeers." Variety, 273 (26 December), 12.
        Film doesn't parody book, but rather adds comedy to its
plot while also showing some of the darker side of 17th Century life.

281   MOTTÉ, MICHÈLE. "Les Douze Mousquetaires [The Twelve Muske-
teers]." L'Express, No. 1146 (25 June), 36-37.
        Comments on the prospects of the as-yet-unreleased The
Three Musketeers and mentions a few previous French versions, in French.

282   SHIVAS, MARK. "Lester's Back and the Musketeers Have Got Him."
New York Times (5 August), Section 2, p. 9.
        Short interviews on location in Spain with Heston, Duna-
way and Lester.

1974

283   ALLEN, TOM. "Top Liner." New York, 7 (30 September), 72.
        Juggernaut is "Lester's most comfortable accommodation
yet with commercial filmmaking," vastly superior to The
Poseidon Adventure. His films have always been "cold, calculated," but have dealt with increasingly intellectual sub-
jects up to The Three Musketeers. Juggernaut is still another kind of film on which Lester has left his distinctive
mark.

284   ANDRÉASON, SVERKER. "De Tre Musketörerna." Chaplin, No. 5,
p. 9.
        Review of The Three Musketeers, in Swedish.

285   ANON. Notice of The Three Musketeers. Films and Filming, 20
(April), 8.
        Film is superior to the previous versions without imi-
tating any of them. The "biggest surprise" is Michael
York's "revelation" of a performance.

286   ANON. "One for All: The New Musketeers." Time, 103 (22
April), 65-66.
        Article sketches Lester's career and describes his free-
wheeling approach to The Three Musketeers--the duels, the
gimmicks, etc.

287   ANON. "Richard Lester's Juggernaut." Films and Filming, 21
          (October), 16-17.
             Photo preview.

288   ANON. "The Three Musketeers." Christian Century, 91 (20
          March), 325.
             Notice calls film a "successful and important comedy
          hit."

289   ANON. "The Three Musketeers." Cineaste, 6:60.
             Notice.

290   ANON. "The Three Musketeers." Senior Scholastic, 104
          (2 May), 21.
             Film is "hilarious, breathless, charming, biting, witty
          and wonderful."

291   ARGUS. "The Musketeers: Diverting, But...." Daily Rag
          [Washington, D.C.], 2 (11 April), 6.
             In The Three Musketeers, Lester depends on the swordplay
          rather than character to carry the action. The film's ini-
          tial multilevel richness is undermined by the surface gags,
          unlike Richardson's Tom Jones, which maintains a darker
          tone even during horseplay.

292   ARMES, ROY. "The Return of Richard Lester." London Magazine,
          14 (December 1974/January 1975), 107-111.
             Lester, a British-based American expatriate, has not
          produced films comparable to those of other countries' ex-
          patriates--Boorman, Forman, Polanski. He peaked in 1964,
          but even then the spontaneity and youthfulness of his style
          was "no more than a pose." When, with How I Won the War,
          he indicated that he wanted to be taken seriously, he fal-
          tered badly. "His qualities and limitations" are revealed
          by The Three Musketeers, which succeeds because it's "all
          froth." Juggernaut fails due to the "imprecision" of Les-
          ter's technique and his lack of regard for the characters.

293   ARNOLD, GARY. "Star-Filled Three Musketeers." Washington
          Post (1 April), Section B, pp. 1, 4.
             This "perfunctory" version of Dumas leaves "little resi-
          dual pleasure." It lacks "suspense and conviction" but is
          sufficiently entertaining for the Saturday matinee crowd.
          The splitting of the story to make a sequel seems unneces-
          sary.

294   AVERY, WILLIAM. "The Three Musketeers." Films in Review, 25
          (April), 248-49.

1974

> Film is "extremely rich and funny," containing a "vitality and esprit" rare in modern adventure films, with a leavening of "social satire."

295 BEARD, BILL. "Disaster Flick Pleasant Change." Poundmaker [Edmonton, Canada], 3 (11 November), 13.
Lester's "nervous" style is "surprisingly apt" for the suspense plot of Juggernaut. He is a technical virtuoso; his film grows in impressiveness as the tension heightens.

296 _____. "Three Musketeers a Comic Spectacle." Poundmaker [Edmonton, Canada], 3 (12 August), 6.
Film is oblivious of everything but its own pace. Characterization is light, and Dumas seems forgotten, or at any rate "sold out for cheap laughs."

297 BILLINGTON, MICHAEL. Notice of The Three Musketeers. Illustrated London News, 262 (July), 87.
Film is "full of slapstick, swordfights and relish for the medium."

298 BOGDANOVICH, PETER. "Period Piece." New York, 7 (25 February), 64-66.
Lester's The Three Musketeers is the best of all the film adaptations of the book, and his best film. He manages to provide action-film thrills and to undercut them ironically without alienating the audience. There is some inobtrusive social commentary, and the political allegory-- the Musketeers have much in common with the Watergate plumbers--is much more successful than that of How I Won the War.

299 BRAUCOURT, GUY and HENRY MORET. "Les Trois Mousquetaires." Écran, 22 (February), 68-69.
Notice describes film as less lively than one would expect from Lester. In French.

300 BRISCOE, BILL. "Three Musketeers a Gem." Iconoclast [Dallas], 8 (5 April), 21.
Lester has "fulfilled the promise" of his early career; he is the best director of comedy since silent days. He, and screenwriter Fraser provide undated Dumasian adventure. The characters resemble those in Buster Keaton's comedies; Keaton always played the "man trying to survive in a universe gone mad," only to be ultimately felled by a blow of fate.

301 BROOKS, RANDY. "Humor, Suspense Keep Juggernaut Afloat." Iconoclast [Dallas], 8 (11 October), 12, 20.

1974

Despite a slight lag near the end of the film, suspense is sustained even as Lester adds "effective" throwaway humor.

302 CANBY, VINCENT. "Juggernaut, Extortion on the High Seas, Opens." New York Times (28 September), p. 26.
Film has no style, no characters, and an awkward screenplay.

303 _____. "Spirited Three Musketeers (No. 6)." New York Times (4 April), p. 52.
Film is generally amusing and interesting, although it is "light on character" and fight sequences lack "spontaneity."

304 COCKS, JAY. "All at Sea." Time, 104 (21 October), 9, 12.
Lester is "a film maker of satiric skill and carbolic wit unsurpassed in the contemporary English-speaking cinema" and a "superb stylist." Juggernaut is predictable, but Lester manages to "obscure the inevitable" in order to create a suspense-filled entertainment.

305 _____. "One for All." Time, 103 (25 March), 68.
The Three Musketeers is "a surfeit of pleasures," which "careens along on its own high spirits." The characters are made human by the absurdity of their heroics, and by their survivor qualities.

306 COLEMAN, JOHN. Review of Juggernaut. New Statesman, 88 (18 October), 549.
Film will "do very well" thanks to "highly intelligent cutting" and the attention paid to Fallon and his crew.

307 _____. Review of The Three Musketeers. New Statesman, 87 (29 March), 458.
Film has a disarming "geniality"; its antic humor "relies on a weird fidelity to its abused original."

308 COMBS, RICHARD. "The Three Musketeers (The Queen's Diamonds)." [BFI] Monthly Film Bulletin, 41 (May), 107-108.
Credits, synopsis, review. Film is a "confident return to form" for Lester, which neatly undercuts the romance with absurdity while leaving the swordplay fairly exciting. The background scenes of low-life and the court intrigues comment on one another. D'Artagnan is the link; he is "occasionally" able to pull off the Fairbanksian acrobatic feats that backfire on the others, and although he shares the "cavalier aspirations" of his friends, his origins are lowly.

1974

309   CORLISS, RICHARD. "A Hard Day's Night: Ten Years After."
       Film Comment, 10 (May), 25.
          Nostalgic reminiscences of the era in which the film ap-
       peared and the effect it had. It retains its grace and
       charm, but the sense of lost youth one feels when re-viewing
       it now makes it melancholy. "It was a glorious rite of
       passage...to nowhere."

310   CRIST, JUDITH. Review of The Three Musketeers. New York, 7
       (8 April), 78.
          Lester updates the story in the best way; he gives it a
       contemporary twist while retaining the elements that dis-
       tinguish its source.

311   CUFF, HASLETT. "Juggernaut: A Worthy Vessel." Georgia
       Straight [Vancouver, Canada], 8? (3 October), 10.
          The film's strength is in its "well-drawn" characters;
       it is "never quite as tensely thrilling as it would like
       to be."

312   _____. "Magnificent Musketeers and Schizoid Disc Jockeys."
       Georgia Straight [Vancouver, Canada], 8? (4 April), 14-15.
          Lester's return with The Three Musketeers is "joyously
       auspicious." Rather than betray the original, he plays
       with it, producing "sheer, unadulterated belly-laughing
       kicks." The cast is "wonderful."

313   DASSINGER, GEORGE. "The Three Musketeers." Aquarian [Passaic,
       N.J.], 8 (11 April), 18, 25.
          The humor and satire are "the keys to the film." The
       earlier Gene Kelly version of the story was fun to watch
       but unbelievable. Lester's has more realism and is more
       faithful to Dumas.

314   FALLOWELL, DUNCAN. "Floodtide." Spectator, 233 (19 October),
       504.
          Juggernaut is reminiscent of the Titanic chronicle, A
       Night to Remember, without its "grandeur."

315   FRANK, ELLEN. Review of The Three Musketeers. Ann Arbor Sun,
       2 (31 May), 25.
          Film is a "major step towards good new comedy." Lester
       has "aged and wised up," adding irony and a wealth of peri-
       od detail to his list of stylistic devices. The swordfights
       are particularly well-done, combining slapstick and athleti-
       cism.

316 FRUMKES, ROY. "Juggernaut." Films in Review, 25 (November),
568-69.
Notice calls film a "quiet disaster film." Compared to
the Hollywood variety, Lester's is witty, human-oriented,
understated.

317 GILLIATT, PENELOPE. Review of The Three Musketeers. New
Yorker, 50 (8 April), 111-12.
The film owes more to Lester and his cast than to Dumas
himself. "The pratfalls and vagaries of flowery speech are
readymade for the beady attentiveness of humorists and
children."

318 GOW, GORDON. "The Three Musketeers." Films and Filming, 20
(May), 47.
Film has beauty and humor. York is successful as both
clown and earnest youth. Aside from very occasional labori-
ousness, Lester keeps the pace lively.

319 _____. "The Three Musketeers." In International Film Guide
1975. Edited by Peter Cowie. London: Tantivy Press;
New York: A. S. Barnes, pp. 157, 159, 168.
Notice.

320 GREEN, BENNY. "Athos, Pathos and Bathos Revisited." Punch,
266 (3 April), 561-62.
The Three Musketeers should be adapted for the screen
"with a straight face," because Dumas provides his own
comedy. Every adaptation, including Lester's, jokes it up,
with gags that are false to Dumas.

321 HALLIWELL, LESLIE. "The Knack." In his The Filmgoer's Companion. New York: Hill and Wang, p. 435.
Notice says that "the film unfortunately encouraged less
talented filmmakers, and even Lester himself, to think that
anything goes providing you keep moving."

322 _____. "Lester, Dick or Richard." In his The Filmgoer's Companion. New York: Hill and Wang, p. 461.
Film list.

323 HARDAWAY, FRANCINE. "The Three Musketeers." New Times [Tempe,
Arizona], 6 (10 April), 11.
Film's pace makes it succeed. Lester doesn't make the
mistake Mel Brooks and Woody Allen make by trying to inter-
ject a message.

1974

324   HATCH, ROBERT. Review of The Three Musketeers. Nation, 218
        (27 April), 540.
            The film is "brainless" fun.

325   HINE, AL. Juggernaut. Toronto, London, and New York: Bantam
        Books, Inc., 201 pp.
            Novelization of screenplay.

326   HOFSESS, JOHN. "The Three Musketeers." Macleans, 87 (June),
        92.
            Notice.

327   INMAN, RICK. "Lester's Juggernaut." Bugle American [Milwau-
        kee], 5 (16 October), 35.
            The screenplay is weak, but Lester redeems the story with
        "parodying swipes," low-key humor, and "visual playfulness."

328   JUNGSTEDT, TORSTEN. "Juggernaut." Chaplin, No. 8, p. 285.
            Review in Swedish.

329   KAEL, PAULINE. Review of Juggernaut. New Yorker, 50 (7 Octo-
        ber), 154-56.
            Characters lack warmth, but have "black-hearted exis-
        tential bravado." Lester's coldbloodedness is "nifty" as
        he undercuts the clichés.

330   KAUFFMANN, STANLEY. Review of The Three Musketeers. New Re-
        public, 170 (27 April), 22, 33.
            Film is "un-Lesterly," "derivative...harmful to Dumas."
        The cinematography seems too lush for the slapstick; the
        characters are robbed of individuality; there is "no sweep,
        no romance, no convincing chivalric tradition to mock."

331   KERNAN, MICHAEL [and MICHAEL YORK]. "Michael York, Alias
        D'Artagnan." Washington Post (1 April), Section B, pp. 1,
        4.
            Short interview deals mostly with The Three Musketeers
        and Lester.

332   KNICKERBOCKER, PAINE. "Lester Rides Wild Again." San Fran-
        cisco Chronicle (29 March), p. 50.
            Review of The Three Musketeers.

333   KORDA, MICHAEL. "Eight-Times a Movie, The Three Musketeers is
        Superb Entertainment." Glamour, 71 (May), 32.
            Lester is a comedic "genius," using "shameless" bits of
        business. The film is a "maniacal tour de force," beauti-
        fully acted, costumed and detailed.

1974

334 _____. "Three Terrific Suspense Movies About Man-Made Disas-
ters--All Starters of a New Genre in Films." Glamour, 72
(December), 173.
Juggernaut transcends the disaster genre because Lester
is interested in people and never lets the situation take
over.

335 LANDAU, JON. "The Three Musketeers." Rolling Stone, No. 158
(11 April), p. 70.
Lester is faithful to the source, but still finds a
fresh approach; satiric but affectionate, with some social
criticism added. He has grown stylistically; most of the
action is "not only brilliant but hilarious."

336 LEAYMAN, CHARLES. "Juggernaut." Lancaster Independent Press,
6 (11 October), 8.
Film is marvelously exciting and "stirring." The characters are human; for Lester the real suspense lies not with
the bombs but with the people's reaction to them. The bombs
make the film exciting, but it is the people, struggling
against life's absurdity in their various ways, that make
it rich.

337 _____. "Lester's Roaring, Happy Three Musketeers Here."
Lancaster Independent Press, 6 (5 April), 8.
The actors are a major factor in the film's excellence;
Lester is another. He has brought off the "impossible mar-
riage" of MGM period dramas and the Keaton-Chaplin comedy
tradition.

338 LOCHTE, DICK. "The Three Musketeers." Los Angeles Free Press,
11 (29 March), 19.
Film has something for everyone: romance, larceny, hon-
or, and Marx Brothers zaniness. Lester's genius "shines"
as he provides "gusto" and inventiveness--the sword play,
for instance, is done as though the actors really don't
know who should be winning.

339 McBRIDE, JOSEPH. "Richard Lester." In International Film
Guide 1975. Edited by Peter Cowie. London: Tantivy Press;
New York: A. S. Barnes, pp. 48-59.
Lester's films are seen in terms of their multilevel com-
plexity and emotional ambivalence (as in The Three Musketeers, where our feeling of superiority over the heroes wars
with our admiration for them). War or social hysteria is
an underlying theme throughout Lester's work. Filmography.

1974

340   McKEE, ALLEN. "A Great Deal of Fun--But Is It Worth Doing?"
      New York Times (14 April), Section 2, p. 13.
            The Three Musketeers is "soulless" and "camp" but none-
      theless effective. Lester should go on to subjects less
      trivial and two-dimensional.

341   MILLAR, GAVIN. "High and Low Adventures." Listener, 92 (24
      October), 537.
            In Juggernaut, Lester knows his audience and its expec-
      tations and somehow manages to inject a little surprise into
      the clichés he knowingly uses.

342   MILLER, EDWIN. "Juggernaut." Seventeen, 33 (December), 35.
            Notice calls direction "sharp, muscular."

343   _____. "Movie of the Month." Seventeen, 33 (May), 53.
            Notice of The Three Musketeers says Lester brings a "de-
      lightfully loony" touch to the story.

344   MINISH, GEOFFREY. "The Three Musketeers." Take One, 4 (22
      January), 32-33.
            Lester's "contempt" covers all classes in the film. His
      style is "dazzling but cheap" and he photographs the female
      stars badly.

345   MINTON, LYNN. "Juggernaut." McCalls, 102 (December), 42.
            Notice says film is tolerable because of the humorous
      touches between tense moments.

346   _____. "The Three Musketeers." McCalls, 101 (May), 85.
            Notice warns that some scenes may upset younger viewers.

347   MONACO, JAMES. "Lester." Mimeographed. New York: Zoetrope
      3, The New School Department of Film.
            Collection of film notes in conjunction with a detailed
      study of Lester and showings of his films. Contains techni-
      cal credits, cast lists, and short but well-researched back-
      ground notes for all the films up to The Bed-Sitting Room.
      Also discusses a few of Lester's commercials.

348   _____. "Some Late Clues to the Lester Direction." Film Com-
      ment, 10 (May), 24-31.
            Discussion and analysis of Lester's work up to the Mus-
      keteers films, synthesizing information from the Gelmis
      (No. 259), Cameron and Shivas (No. 202), and McBride (No.
      279) interviews and adding a great deal of intelligent,
      original thought. Lester's one consistent flaw is his some-
      what off-putting show of intellect which makes some of his
      films "more thought-about than felt."

349   MURF. "Juggernaut." Variety, 276 (18 September), 19.
        Lester creates "moderate" human interest and "fair" sus-
      pense. The dramatic potential is undermined by restrained
      filming and underplayed acting.

350   NELSON, LIZA. "The Three Musketeers." Great Speckled Bird
        [Atlanta], 7 (15 April), 15.
        Film is a "major disappointment" due to the "simple-
      minded" plot, the lack of characterization and of social
      commentary. The film is "weak, superficial humor wrapped
      in technically inferior cinematography."

351   OSTER, JERRY. "Musketeers Clever But Tedious." New York Daily
        News (4 April), p. 114.
        Review of The Three Musketeers.

352   OVERBEY, DAVID L. "The Three Musketeers." Sight and Sound,
        43 (Spring), 116-17.
        The film is fragmented not, as usual, by Lester's editing
      style, but by his "anarchic" humor. He runs risks by ridi-
      culing the romances in the story, and he sometimes loses,
      but the film is his "best work in years."

353   PERLMUTTER, GARY. "Some High Points." Valley Advocate [Am-
        herst, Massachusetts], 2 (11 December), 25, 34.
        Notice calls The Three Musketeers "precise," well-acted
      and well-executed.

354   PERRY, GEORGE. "Dick Lester." In his The Great British Pic-
        ture Show. New York: Hill and Wang, pp. 241-43, 318-19.
        Brief survey of the films up to The Bed-Sitting Room,
      filmographical listing.

355   POLMAN, JEFFREY. "The Three Musketeers." Valley Advocate
        [Amherst, Massachusetts], 1 (29 May), 15.
        Film is confused, tedious, all costume. York is "the
      worst comic actor since Mussolini."

356   POWELL, DILYS. "Bang On Target." Sunday Times [London] (31
        March), p. 35.
        In The Three Musketeers, Lester has a "feeling for the
      bravado...and the gusto" of the cinematic past. The actors
      are all fine, as is the cinematography. The film "may not
      look serious; but I think its style and mood are to be taken
      seriously."

357   _____. Review of Juggernaut. Sunday Times [London] (13 Octo-
        ber), p. 33.

1974

>   The "detail of the script and the smartness of the direc-
> tion" distract the audience's attention from the film's
> predictability.

358   RAINER, PETER. "Juggernaut." Mademoiselle, 80 (December),
>   104.
>   Notice calls film "clap-trap," "routine and humorless."

359   REED, REX. "A Classy Re-Entry for Miss Chaplin." Washington
>   Post (21 April), Section E, pp. 1, 5.
>   Article on Geraldine Chaplin calls her performance in
>   The Three Musketeers a "luminescent natural pearl in a wash-
>   tub of noisy and nacreous oyster shells." The film itself
>   is "idiotic."

360   RENAUD, TRISTAN. "Les Trois Mousquetaires." Cinéma, No. 84
>   (February), p. 101.
>   The film lacks personality, notably Lester's. In French.

361   RICH, FRANK. Review of Juggernaut. New Times, 2 (1 November),
>   57, 62.
>   Compares film with The Taking of Pelham 1-2-3. They both
>   end with a "dramatic...thud." Lester's film is the "clas-
>   sier," containing some of his typical touches.

362   _____. Review of The Three Musketeers. New Times, 2 (5 April),
>   62.
>   Film is a visual "high," but the slapstick is "dumb" and
>   the "loony" peripheral humor has diminished.

363   RICHARD, JEFFREY and ALLEN EYLES. "The Three Musketeers."
>   Focus on Film, No. 18 (Summer), pp. 4-6.
>   The disappearance of the swashbuckler from the screen
>   was unfortunate; Lester has returned it with style. The
>   Three Musketeers is "true to the spirit of the swashbuckler,"
>   affectionately sending-up heroics without ridiculing them.
>   The fights are inventive and imaginatively staged. Most of
>   the lead actors do their turns stylishly; the actresses, ex-
>   cept for Geraldine Chaplin, are unremarkable. Michael York
>   as D'Artagnan is "worthy to stand beside Doug Fairbanks and
>   Gene Kelly." Credits, filmography listing many previous
>   versions.

364   RIPP, JUDITH. "Juggernaut." Parents' Magazine, 49 (November),
>   18.
>   Notice says film lacks suspense and soap-opera style
>   human interest.

1974

365   _____. "The Three Musketeers." <u>Parents' Magazine</u>, 49 (May),
       14.
           Notice calls film "spirited," although Lester uses his
       cast "superficially."

366   ROBINSON, DAVID. Review of <u>Juggernaut</u>. <u>The Times</u> [London]
       (11 October), p. 17.
           Film is a feat of engineering, as opposed to a work of
       art; it is "a well-machined piece of entertainment."

367   _____. "Richard Lester Recovers the Knack." <u>The Times</u> [Lon-
       don] (29 March), p. 12.
           <u>The Three Musketeers</u> is the "revitalization" of Lester.
       His decision to "take the story line straight but swift,
       and centre the action on a strong d'Artagnan" allows wide
       comedic variations.

368   RONAN, MARGARET. "<u>Juggernaut</u>." <u>Senior Scholastic</u>, 105 (14
       November), 24.
           The film's frequent breaks in tension make it seem "made-
       for-TV."

369   ROSENBAUM, JONATHAN. "<u>Juggernaut</u>." [BFI] <u>Monthly Film Bulle-
       tin</u>, 41 (October), 224-25.
           Credits, synopsis, review. This film is more single-
       minded than Lester's other films, unlike <u>The Three Muske-
       teers</u>, which tried to please every audience. This one
       focuses on Fallon and minimizes the several potential sub-
       plots as it maintains a tolerable suspense level.

370   SCHOBER, SIEGFRIED. "Musketiere als Beatles [Musketeers as
       Beatles]." <u>Der Spiegel</u>, 28 (7 January), 89-90.
           Review of <u>The Three Musketeers</u>, in German.

371   SHALES, TOM. "Rejuvenating a Film Genre." <u>Washington Post</u>
       (27 September), Section B, p. 13.
           Lester's wit turns <u>Juggernaut</u>'s "hackneyed" plot into
       "fairly breathless adventure," with the help of a "fine,
       rational script" and a lack of melodrama.

372   SHALIT, GENE. "The Wild Threesome." <u>Ladies' Home Journal</u>,
       91 (June), 4.
           Notice calls <u>The Three Musketeers</u> "the kind of movie for
       which the word 'romp' was coined."

373   SISKEL, GENE. "Dynamite Pacing in <u>Juggernaut</u>." <u>Chicago
       Tribune</u> (1 October), Section 3, p. 5.
           The film is far removed from usual Hollywood disaster
       movies--witty and fast-paced until a very abrupt denouement.

1974

374 SISKEL, GENE. "Three Musketeers." Chicago Tribune (2 April),
Section 2, p. 4.
Film is "a bore from start to finish." The jokes are revealed before they happen, or are overstated; the violence
is tedious.

375 SKINNER, MARGO. Notice of The Three Musketeers. San Francisco Phoenix, 2 (18 April), 5.
Film is "dull, badly-photographed."

376 SMITH, LIZ. "All for One, One for All." Cosmopolitan, 176
(May), 84.
Lester's "whimsy and kinky humor" make The Three Muske-
teers a "delightful romp."

377 SOLVATO, LARRY. "Absurdity for All and All for Craziness."
Westport Trucker [Kansas City, Missouri], 4 (5 April), 17.
After going through a successful initial period, and a
"pretentious" later one, Lester is back, with The Three
Musketeers, "in fine form," and "maturing in style." His
origins go back to the Sennett-Chaplin-Keaton tradition:
the same techniques they used are still working for him.

378 STERRITT, DAVID. "En Garde! The Three Musketeers Are Here."
Christian Science Monitor [Eastern edition], 66 (2 May), F6.
"There's much to watch" in the film, but it lacks the
characters that "turned Dumas's work into a great novel."
Lester does remain true to the author in two ways: he reminds us that the Musketeers were sometimes "losers" as
well as "supermen"; and he refuses "to draw his characters
as wholly good or wholly bad."

379 _____. "A Special Flair for Suspense." Christian Science
Monitor [Eastern edition], 67 (4 December), 10.
Lester's clever direction and "some sterling performances" make Juggernaut a "nifty bit of what's-gonna-happen-
next moviemaking."

380 SUPRYNOWICZ, VIN. "Juggernaut." Valley Advocate [Amherst,
Massachusetts], 2 (9 October), 17.
Film's promotion as a disaster flick cheats both the
audience and Lester and his crew. It is an intimate bomb-
disposal movie, with the conflict centering on the wills
of Juggernaut and Fallon.

381 TERRY, CARROLL. "The Three Musketeers." Good Housekeeping,
178 (May), 56.
Notice calls film "fast-moving and amusing," although
possibly too sophisticated for youngsters.

1974

382   THOMAS, KEVIN. "A Swashbuckling Opening for Filmex." <u>Los</u>
<u>Angeles Times</u> (28 March), Section 4, pp. 1, 20.
Review of <u>The Three Musketeers</u>.

383   VOLK, KATIE. "Musketeer Madness." <u>Express</u> [Hicksville, N.Y.],
2 (4 April), 15.
<u>The Three Musketeers</u> "lacks a certain continuity in the
classic sense," but its "inspired comedy is consistent
throughout." One of Lester's best tricks is using "more
serious...film personalities" by making farcical their "in-
stitutional image."

384   WAGNER, RICHARD [and MICHAEL YORK]. "An Interview With Michael
York." <u>Drummer</u> [Philadelphia], No. 288 (26 March), p. 8.
York discusses, among other things, the accidents, prob-
lems, etc., encountered during the filming of <u>The Three</u>
<u>Musketeers</u>.

385   WALKER, ALEXANDER. <u>Hollywood U. K.</u> New York: Stein and Day,
pp. 221-42, 261-71, 363-65.
Pp. 221-42 discuss Lester's early career and, inciden-
tally, his musical sense as it applies to his films; his
TV work in the 50's, culminating in the <u>Goon Shows</u>; and the
making of <u>A Hard Day's Night</u>, with quotes from the author's
interviews with Lester, producer Shenson, scriptwriter Owen,
cinematographer Taylor. Pp. 261-71 deal with <u>The Knack</u> and
<u>Help!</u> at some length; pp. 363-65 discuss <u>How I Won the War</u>.

386   WALSH, MOIRA. "<u>Juggernaut</u>." <u>America</u>, 131 (12 October), 195.
Film is enhanced by its "urbane" wit and its lack of
melodramatic subplots and of graphic violence, but it may
put off "no-nonsense action fans."

387   WESTERBECK, COLIN L., JR. "Fun for All and All for Fun."
<u>Commonweal</u>, 100 (24 May), 284-85.
This version of <u>The Three Musketeers</u> is a bit "jaded":
the Musketeers are stripped of their ideals; the pratfall
is the driving force behind the film; there is almost an
overabundance of period detail. However, also present is
"Lester's special, ingenious instinct for the pure oafish-
ness in life."

388   _____. "Hijackers and Hijinx." <u>Commonweal</u>, 101 (1 November),
110-111.
In both <u>Juggernaut</u> and <u>The Taking of Pelham 1-2-3</u>, the
criminal attacks the "system" that protects people from
crime rather than the people themselves. Neither film
really has a hero, since the protagonists are basically
passive.

99

1974

389 WHITEHORN, ETHEL. "The Three Musketeers." PTA Magazine, 68
       (June), 5.
          Notice says this "endearing" version of the story is done
       with "great panache, good humor, and disjointed grace."

390 WINE, BILL. "Juggernaut." Drummer [Philadelphia], No. 316
       (8 October), p. 17.
          Lester does a "creditable" directing job despite his
       avoidance of pathos-milking situations.

391 _____. "The Three Musketeers." Drummer [Philadelphia], No.
       288 (26 March), p. 14.
          The film successfully "celebrates and satirizes its
       genre." Direction, cast and production are all at full
       energy; Lester's style has "mellowed"--the humor comes from
       the mise-en-scène rather than the editing.

392 ZIMMERMAN, PAUL D. "Hijack Hijinks." Newsweek, 84 (7 October),
       95.
          The Taking of Pelham 1-2-3 is "pedestrian" compared to
       Juggernaut, whose imagery is beautiful and gives a real
       feeling of a huge ocean liner. The bomb itself is "ele-
       gantly" convincing.

393 _____. "One for All." Newsweek, 83 (15 April), 103.
          In The Three Musketeers, Lester seems to want to "vault
       into high camp," but is forced to stick to the story despite
       his "disbelief."

                          1975

394 ANDREWS, RENA. "Royal Flash Is Big Fizzle." Denver Post
       (13 November). Calls movie "disjointed," with unsustained
       action and disconnected plot. [NB, Card 77.]

395 ANON. "Flash Is a Royal Treat." Florida Times Union [Jackson-
       ville] (23 November).
          The comedic situations in Royal Flash are "imaginative,"
       the cast is "superlative." [NB, Card 77.]

396 ANON. "The Four Musketeers." Los Angeles Free Press, 12 (21
       March), 27.
          The sequel lacks the charm of the first film due to the
       absence of character development and "emotional progres-
       sion."

1975

397   ANON. "The Four Musketeers." St. Louis Post-Dispatch (21
       March).
              Film is "not quite so funny" and clever as The Three, al-
       though still delightful. [NB, Card 17.]

398   ANON. "The Four Musketeers." State Journal-Register [Spring-
       field, Illinois] (12 April).
              Film lacks "a good story" and contains many faults, one
       of which is the wasting of dramatic potential. [NB, Card
       17.]

399   ANON. "The Four Musketeers (The Revenge of Milady)." Films
       and Filming, 21 (February), 30-33.
              Photo preview.

400   ANON. "Four Musketeers Worthy Successor to Three Film." Ore-
       gonian [Portland] (10 April).
              One of the pleasures of the first film was that so much
       money and effort could be spent on a comedy. The lack of
       surprise in this matter is one of The Four Musketeers' prob-
       lems. The other is that the second half of the Dumas story
       doesn't suit Lester's style as well as the first half did,
       although he seems to want to cheer things up. [NB, Card
       17.]

401   ANON. "Holiday Movie Royal Flash Enhances Idiot Box's Appeal."
       News and Observer [Raleigh, N.C.] (26 November).
              Among the film's faults are Lester's lack of comic tim-
       ing, the "pedestrian" script, and undistinguished acting.
       [NB, Card 77.]

402   ANON. "Juggernaut." Cineaste, 6:52.
              Notice.

403   ANON. Review of The Four Musketeers. Playboy, 22 (May), 26.

404   ANON. "Royal Flash." El Paso Times [Texas] (30 November).
              Film is an extension of the Musketeer duology and as
       such has nothing "new or refreshing" to offer. [NB, Card
       77.]

405   ANON. "Royal Flash a Great Success." Metro-East Journal
       [East St. Louis, Illinois] (23 November).
              Film is satisfying on all counts, particularly as a con-
       tinuation of the teaming of Lester and George Macdonald
       Fraser. [NB, Card 77.]

1975

406   ANON. "Royal Flash Is a Rousing Farce." Sun [Baltimore] (27
        October).
            This film is superior to the Musketeers movies--fresher,
        less ponderous, and visually beautiful. [NB, Card 63.]

407   ANON. "Second Section Musketeers Here." Dallas Morning News
        (21 March).
            The Four Musketeers is "almost as funny" as The Three,
        taking into consideration the heavier subject matter. [NB,
        Card 17.]

408   ANON. [and RICHARD LESTER]. "Where the M3 Joins the M4."
        Films Illustrated, 4 (April), 296-97.
            Background article on The Four Musketeers, quoting Les-
        ter extensively on the "agony" of filmmaking.

409   ANSEN, DAVID. "Buckled Swash." Real Paper [Boston], 4 (19
        November), 32.
            Royal Flash is "tiresome" and ill-conceived.

410   ARNOLD, GARY. "An Engrossing Four Musketeers." Washington
        Post (19 March), Section B, pp. 1, 7.
            The two films would have been better as one epic; as
        they stand they are "entertaining but oddly incongruous";
        the first is all action, the second all exposition. Reed
        and Dunaway are "impressive" as they dominate the sequel.

411   _____. "Royal Flash." Washington Post (25 October), Section
        A, p. 18.
            Lester's "heart isn't in it." He and others have done
        everything in the film before.

412   BANKS, DICK. "Musketeers Is One for All." Charlotte Observer
        [North Carolina] (24 March).
            The Four Musketeers is more of the same, although Duna-
        way almost steals the show. [NB, Card 17.]

413   BATDORFF, EMERSON. "Royal Flash Is a Flub." Plain Dealer
        [Cleveland] (23 October).
            Film is labored; Lester is too "insistent" in trying for
        laughs. [NB, Card 63.]

414   BEAVEN, SCOTT. "Musketeers Sequel Just Same Stuff." Albu-
        querque Journal (20 March).
            Movie is "the second half of Richard Lester's embarras-
        sing pratfall orgy" and the "biggest comedown for a major
        artist" since Chaplin "made a senile fool of himself" with
        A Countess from Hong Kong. [NB, Card 17.]

415   BENAYOUN, ROBERT. "Richard Lester Dans Son Bloc d'Ambre."
Positif, No. 175 (November), pp. 42-48.
Long examination of The Bed-Sitting Room, the thwarted
projects of the following five years, The Three and The
Four Musketeers, Juggernaut, Royal Flash, and, briefly, the
forthcoming Robin and Marian. In French.

416   _____, MICHEL CIMENT [and RICHARD LESTER]. "Deux Entretiens
Avec Richard Lester [Two Interview with Richard Lester]."
Positif, No. 175 (November), pp. 31-41.
Superior, non-repetitive interview deals with the films
from The Three Musketeers to Robin and Marian. Lester discusses at some length his approach to adapting Dumas and
his casting of the film, as well as detailing the historical
research involved. He also discusses the state of British
filmmaking, Buster Keaton, and possible future projects.
In French.

417   BIELECKI, STANLEY, comp. "Royal Flash." Films and Filming,
21 (May), 29-32.
Picture preview.

418   BILLINGTON, MICHAEL. Review of Royal Flash. Illustrated London News, 263 (September), 82.
Film is a "heavy-handed mistake."

419   BLANK, EDWARD L. "Four Musketeers Funnier Than Three." Pittsburgh Press (27 March).
The film manages to incorporate some "tragic plot twists"
without ruining the comic tone. [NB, Card 17.]

420   BOND, SPIKE. "Royal Flash." Films Illustrated, 4 (August),
463.
Reader's letter, pointing out deficiencies, inconsis-
tencies, and a few good spots in the movie.

421   BOWERS, RONALD. "Royal Flash." Films in Review, 26 (November), 568-69.
Notice calls film "sophomoric, unevenly paced, and
silly."

422   BROOKS, RANDY. "The Four Musketeers Part II Is Tragic Comedy."
Iconoclast [Dallas], 9 (4 April), 13, 20.
The film is moderately amusing and involving. Many of
the bits--goonish mutterings, "fiendish thingies," etc.--
are familiar from the Beatles films.

1975

423   BROWN, GEOFF. "The Four Musketeers." Sight and Sound, 44
       (Spring), 124-25.
            This is "all too plainly half a film," troubled by
       several false endings. There are fewer gags, some of which
       are used for dramatic effect. Dumas loses his dignity but
       retains his panache as the "quizzical" incidental survey
       of the 17th century continues, displaying Lester's newly
       acquired restraint and coherence of style.

424   CAIN, SCOTT. "Dual Musketeers Pale, Alas." Atlanta Journal
       (28 March).
            The Four Musketeers has "its fair share" of excitement
       and fun, but it seems like a leftover from The Three. [NB,
       Card 17.]

425   CANBY, VINCENT. "Four Cheers for Lester's Light-Headed Mus-
       keteers." New York Times (20 March), p. 48.
            The Four Musketeers is "lighter, funnier, less burdened
       by exposition" than The Three.

426   _____. "Lester's Royal Flash Opens." New York Times (11 Oc-
       tober), p. 23.
            Film is "good comic fun" in which Lester "throws away
       more gags than some comedy directors think up in an entire
       career." He is sometimes free with his comedy at the ex-
       pense of the total film.

427   CARROLL, KATHLEEN. "Flash-and-Dash Foolishness." New York
       Daily News (11 October).
            Direction and acting in Royal Flash are partly to blame
       for its being a "dull-witted bore" and a "waste of talent."
       [NB, Card 63.]

428   CASTELL, DAVID. "The Four Musketeers." Films Illustrated, 4
       (April), 284.
            The film is darker in tone than its predecessor, fit-
       tingly. The shift of focus from d'Artagnan to Athos allows
       several of the actors enlarged scope.

429   CHAMPLIN, CHARLES. "Royal Flash." Las Vegas Review-Journal
       (11 October).
            Film is a "thin story, marvelously illustrated." Mc-
       Dowell is "too unconcealably modern" as Flashman, neither
       a hero nor an antihero. [NB, Card 63.]

430   CHERNIN, DONNA. "Four Musketeers Follows Up on Exploits of
       Three." Plain Dealer [Cleveland] (22 March).

The two parts of the original long film are not interesting enough to justify splitting them. The second film is inferior to the first, and both are inferior to the book. [NB, Card 17.]

431 COCKS, JAY. "Rogues' Gallery." Time, 106 (20 October), 62, 64.
Most of the humor in Royal Flash comes from Flashman's weak character and is quickly exhausted. The satire fails, and the direction is strangely uninspired.

432 COLEMAN, JOHN. Notice of The Four Musketeers. New Statesman, 89 (28 March), 425.
The film "looks perfectly splendid" but "inevitably suffers from our previous experience of The Three Musketeers."

433 ____. Review of Royal Flash. New Statesman, 90 (11 July), 61.
From a promising start, the plot goes in too many directions, the humor bogs down too many times.

434 CRIST, JUDITH. Review of The Four Musketeers. New York, 8 (31 March), 66-67.
The emphasis is changed from the action of the first to characterization. Each musketeer gains individuality, as does the rest of the cast. The result is "less raucous" but "more satisfying."

435 ____. Review of Royal Flash. Saturday Review, 3 (1 November), 48-49.
After his treatment of Dumas, Lester's ideas in this film seem stale. All the characters "seem fragmented, as if their major moments were edited out."

436 CUFF, HASLETT. "More Sanguine Swashbuckling." Georgia Straight [Vancouver, Canada], 9 (3 April), 10, 23.
The Four Musketeers contains "much of the same" as the "brilliant" first film, but the tone is darker, "there is reckoning to be paid." Reprinted in Lancaster Independent Press, 7 (18 April), 8.

437 ____. Review of Royal Flash. Georgia Straight [Vancouver, Canada], 9 (30 October), 15.
The film is diverting; everything is done right. However, too much of it has already been done in the Musketeers films; "Lester is running on recycled inspiration."

1975

438 CUSKELLY, RICHARD. "Derring-Do Minus Romance." Los Angeles Herald-Examiner (9 October).
Compares Royal Flash with Musketeers films, using contrasts between the characters and ideologies of d'Artagnan and Flashman to illustrate the point that the latter is less at home in the romantic adventure genre than the former. [NB, Card 63.]

439 DAVIS, RUSSELL E. "The Four Musketeers--Slightly Tragic Slap-Stick." Jump-Cut, No. 8 (August/September), p. 10.
The humor in the sequel is decidedly dark, as war is waged and featured actors are killed off; social satire about the 1620's is difficult because it was a very unfunny period. York, Reed and Dunaway dominate the film as their characters develop.

440 DIETRICH, JEAN. "Acting Keeps Royal Flash From Failing." Courier-Journal [Louisville, Kentucky] (31 October).
The acting of McDowell, Reed and Bates overcomes "heavy-handed" material. [NB, Card 63.]

441 DREW, BERNARD. "Four Musketeers--Easy-to-Take Film." Rochester Democrat and Chronicle (20 March).
Film is amusing but not "inspired." [NB, Card 17.]

442 EBERT, ROGER. "More Manic Musketeers." Chicago Sun-Times (26 March).
The Three and The Four Musketeers are "too much of the same stuff." The characters are not made real enough to involve the audience; however, everything is nice to look at--"the movie does have a nice, slick surface as simple linear diversion." [NB, Card 17.]

443 _____. "One Musketeer Film Too Many." Chicago Sun-Times (13 October).
Royal Flash is more of the same stuff as the Musketeers films. It has a disturbing ambiguity of tone as it intermingles gags and violence. Both the actors, and other aspects of the total production, seem "unfocused." [NB, Card 63.]

444 EICHELBAUM, STANLEY. "A Flash In the Pan Comedy." San Francisco Examiner (9 October).
Royal Flash is "laborious" and heavy-handed; its cast is uninspired. [NB, Card 63.]

445 ENGVÉN, INGVAR. "De Fyra Musketörerna." Chaplin, 17 (No. 1), 6.
Review of The Four Musketeers, in Swedish.

446 EYQUEM, OLIVIER. "Biofilmographie de Richard Lester." Posi-
      tif, No. 175 (November), pp. 48-52.
          Résumé, in French, of Lester's life, career and TV work
      up to It's Trad, Dad. Thorough filmography through Robin
      and Marian. References to other articles on Lester that
      have appeared in Positif.

447 FARREN, JONATHAN. "Royal Flash--Lester Ressuscité?" Cinéma,
      No. 204 (December), pp. 133-34.
          Film has the "mordant verve of the novels of Fielding
      and Thackeray, renewed with films like Tony Richardson's
      Tom Jones or Karel Reisz's Morgan." Lester has been prema-
      turely considered dead as a filmmaker. In French.

448 FINOCCHIARO, RAY. "Musketeers Back on Film with Fights, Vis-
      tas and Fun." Wilmington Evening Journal [Delaware] (27
      March).
          The Four Musketeers is less bogged down with "plot me-
      chanics" than The Three, though filled with "outrageous"
      but "devilishly clever" visual gags. [NB, Card 17.]

449 _____. "Royal Flash Fails to Ignite." Wilmington Evening
      Journal [Delaware] (24 October).
          Both the gags and the film itself run out of steam pre-
      maturely. [NB, Card 63.]

450 FLOOD, RICHARD. "Something of a Pan for the Flash." Drummer
      [Philadelphia], No. 372 (28 October), p. 10.
          Royal Flash should have worked from old films, rather
      than from Fraser's book; still, it is "watchable" and most
      of the cast does well--particularly Bates, who brings a
      "fascinating" ambiguity to his character.

451 GAGNARD, FRANK. "Musketeers Time." Times-Picayune [New Or-
      leans] (24 March).
          The Four Musketeers is merely more of the same, with no
      visual or stylistic surprises. [NB, Card 17.]

452 GALLIGAN, RICHARD. "Flashman is Pushy." New Haven Register
      [Connecticut] (2 November).
          In Royal Flash, Lester's cleverness works against him,
      becoming "manic." The film refuses to commit itself to
      being either a swashbuckler or a parody of one. The cast,
      except for Bates, is unconvincing. [NB, Card 73.]

453 GALLO, WILLIAM. "Lester's Musketeers Still Travel Raffish
      Road." Denver Post (24 March).

1975

The Four Musketeers continues in the same vein as its
predecessor, skilfully and freshly offering glimpses of
both the absurd and the dark side of Dumas. [NB, Card 17.]

454 _____. "Royal Flash a Mid-Atlantic Comedy Based in Bavaria."
Rocky Mountain News [Denver] (13 November).
McDowell is responsible for the film's best moments, but
it lacks the "cutting edge" and the "lunatic purity" the
same material might have had in the hands of Ken Russell or
Stanley Kubrick. [NB, Card 77.]

455 GARDNER, R. H. "The Same Gang Is Back." Sun [Baltimore] (4
April).
The Four Musketeers is "the same movie" as The Three;
the problem with both is that comedy mixes with melodrama
so that their mood is uncertain. [NB, Card 17.]

456 GILLIATT, PENELOPE. Review of The Four Musketeers. New York-
er, 51 (31 March), 79-81.
Film is fragmented, rich in detail and visual humor.
However, the fragmentation sometimes obstructs the humor.
The "try-anything-once" rapid-fire jokes don't build.

457 GOLDSTEIN, RUTH M. "A Hard Day's Night." Film News, 32 (No-
vember/December), 24.
There are too few good zany comedies to allow this one
to be relegated to "oldie" status. It is also of interest
to modern viewers who have followed the Beatles' career and
musical development.

458 GOW, GORDON. "The Four Musketeers." Films and Filming, 21
(April), 37.
Faye Dunaway is the main attraction in the second half
of the duology. Effective use is made of images and sounds.
Despite the shift in emphasis, this film is "every bit as
exhilarating as its predecessor."

459 _____. "Royal Flash." Films and Filming, 21 (September), 36.
Lester's "zest" and McDowell's performance keep the
comedy going, "shot with subserious glints."

460 _____ [and MALCOLM McDOWELL]. "Something More." Films and
Filming, 22 (October), 10-16.
Long interview with McDowell includes comments on Royal
Flash and his approach to the Flashman character.

461 GRANT, PAUL. "The Four Musketeers." Ann Arbor Sun, 3 (9 May),
18.

108

1975

The film is different from The Three in that "people die." While there is still fun, "it is shrewd and devastating cinema, which with a few sharp strokes brings down the intricate fantasy castles of its predecessor."

462 GREEN, BENNY. "Not A. Hope." Punch, 269 (16 July), 109.
Fraser's script for Royal Flash fails where his novel almost works as romantic pastiche. In order to score off melodrama, farce must be played straight to heighten the humor. Thus, Royal Flash should have been a straight remake of The Prisoner of Zenda except for the Flashman character.

463 GUARINO, ANN. "Big Swashbuckler." New York Daily News (20 March).
The Four Musketeers has less slapstick and more swashbuckle than the first film, while retaining Lester's "light touch" and attention to detail. [NB, Card 17.]

464 HARDAWAY, FRANCINE. "The Four Musketeers." New Times [Tempe, Arizona], 6 (9 April), 13.
Since the film is a continuation of The Three, and thus a series of climaxes, it seems bloodier. Motivations stated in the first film aren't restated here, so this film is unfairly "trivialized."

465 HARDWICK, MICHAEL. The Four Musketeers. New York: Bantam Books, Inc., 122 pp.
Novel based on the original screenplay. Of interest in comparing earlier ideas with finished film (which differs markedly in spots from this novel).

466 HOFSESS, JOHN. "How I Learned to Stop Worrying and Love Disasters." Macleans, 88 (January), 68.
Notice of Juggernaut in an article that discusses 1974's trend toward sequels and disaster films. Lester's film is the most sophisticated of its genre; the pace, characterization and acting improve the "mindless premise."

467 _____. "Recommended." Macleans, 88 (May), 96.
Notice calls The Four Musketeers an "infectious mixture of ribaldry and zany cynicism."

468 HOLLANDER, DAVE. "Royal Flash in the Pan." Aquarian [Montclair, N.J.], 10 (22 October), 33.
Misdirection, a weak screenplay and repetitious gags combine to make the film sumptuously "boring."

1975

469   HUDDY, JOHN. "Musketeers Funny, But Repetitious." Miami
          Herald (28 March).
              The Four Musketeers is as meticulously crafted as The
          Three, but lacks its "cavalier absurdity." The beautiful
          camera work stands out above the "improvised" script and
          ungraceful cutting. [NB, Card 17.]

470   _____. "Quite By Accident...a New Musketeers." Miami Herald
          (30 March).
              Includes background information on the origin of the
          double Musketeers saga, and remarks by York and Christopher
          Lee about incidents during filming. [NB, Card 17.]

471   INMAN, RICK. Review of The Four Musketeers. Bugle American
          [Milwaukee], 6 (16 April), 19.
              Film is "far greater" than the first, as Lester uses a
          "much grander mock-heroic style" to portray the triviality
          of the causes for war and the cold-bloodedness of the Mus-
          keteers as they fight it.

472   JACOB, GILLES. "Terreur Sur le 'Britannic.'" L'Express, No.
          1227 (13 January), p. 6.
              Notice, in French, says that Juggernaut shows that in-
          telligence and commercial cinema need not be incompatible.

473   JAMES, HUGH. "The 4 Musketeers." Films in Review, 26 (May),
          312.
              Film is better than The Three, as it combines comedy,
          dramatic tension, and a "brilliant" final duel.

474   JOHNSON, MALCOLM L. "Richard Lester's Four Musketeers." Hart-
          ford Courant [Connecticut] (23 March).
              Film is less brilliant than the first but more meaning-
          ful. Lester cleverly juxtaposes violence and religion--the
          religious war, Milady's nun disguise, the duel in the con-
          vent, etc. [NB, Card 17.]

475   KAEL, PAULINE. Review of Royal Flash. New Yorker, 51 (13 Oc-
          tober), 112-14.
              The film would succeed if the audience could sympathize
          with Flashman. Lester needs to "rediscover simplicity"
          "even more than Ken Russell." Both "overvalue their own
          fertility" but with Russell one senses his relish of "lit-
          tle-boy naughty jokes" while Lester "has no relish left."
          In the Musketeers films he seemed to be combining Keaton's
          love of visual detail with his own of "scurrilous excess"--
          but Royal Flash is disjointed in many areas, and downright
          "nasty" in others. He uses actors "as objects," miscasting

and misusing them. His inventiveness is becoming "desperate."

476 KORDA, MICHAEL. "More Fun with Four Musketeers." Glamour, 73 (June), 92.
       Notice.

477 LEAYMAN, CHARLES D. "Royal Flash." Lancaster Independent Press, 7 (27 November), 10.
       The characters are "cardboard" and the action seems pointless. The entire film seems afflicted with a "meanness of spirit."

478 McELFRESH, TOM. "Extra Musketeer Adds Only Weight." Cincinnati Enquirer (21 March).
       Compared to The Three, The Four Musketeers has a "diminished" look and "takes itself far too seriously." [NB, Card 17.]

479 _____. "Lester's Royal Flash Fizzles Out Fast." Cincinnati Enquirer (24 October).
       Film is "between" in styles, attitudes, interpretations, characterizations; it is neither comedy, adventure, nor romance, but an uneasy blend of all three. [NB, Card 63.]

480 McKINNON, GEORGE. "Four Musketeers Is Too Many." Boston Globe (22 March).
       Film is "too much of a good thing"; it looks as if it were made of leftovers from The Three. [NB, Card 17.]

481 MARZELLA, MICHAEL. "Musketeers Carve Swath of Slapstick." St. Petersburg Times (31 March).
       Although The Four Musketeers contains much death, most of it seems unreal. There is almost no character development aside from the Athos-Milady relationship. [NB, Card 17.]

482 _____. "Royal Flash Comes Up with Belly Laughs." St. Petersburg Times (24 November).
       The film contains "near-brilliant comic twists" but gaps between jokes. It is not hilarious, but rather steadily amusing. [NB, Card 77.]

483 MASLIN, JANET. "More Is Less in Lester's Sequel." Boston Phoenix, 4 (1 April), Section 2, p. 2.
       The real reason for the splitting of the Dumas story must be that the two halves don't "dovetail." In The Four Musketeers, the heroes' cold-blooded treatment of the Huguenots

1975

undermines our sympathy for them and leaves a "gaping hole" in the center of the story.

484 MASTROIANNI, TONY. "Two Cheers for Four Musketeers." Cleveland Press (21 March).
The faults and virtues of this film are much the same as those of the first, although there is a little less light comedy and a little more action and death. [NB, Card 17.]

485 MILLAR, SYLVIA. "Royal Flash." [BFI] Monthly Film Bulletin, 42 (August), 182.
Credits, synopsis, review which says that Lester "dissipates his assets"--his actors, period detail and locations-- into a mere "assembly of clever set-pieces." The lack of suspense slackens the pace; except for some witty dialog, the film is "entertaining...but immediately forgettable."

486 MILLS, DONIA. "Royal Flash: Regal Props, Familiar Gags." Washington Star-News [D.C.] (24 October).
Film is "vacuous." The characters are repulsive, the jokes heavy-handed, and the whole thing repetitive. [NB, Card 63.]

487 MINTON, LYNN. "The Four Musketeers." McCalls, 102 (June), 68.
Notice warns that the film may be less desirable for younger children to see than its predecessor was, since the violence becomes crueler and "closer to us."

488 _____. "Royal Flash." McCalls, 103 (December), 48.
Notice recommends film for age 13 and over, due less to the violence, which is "slapstick," than to Flashman's off-beat womanizing.

489 MITCHELL, MARTIN. Review of The Four Musketeers. After Dark, 8 (May), 89-90.
Film is "funny in a fresh, thoughtfully surrealistic way."

490 _____. Review of Royal Flash. After Dark, 8 (November), 94.
The film looks "hastily assembled." There are clever Lesterian moments but too much swordplay and "stylistic inconsistency."

491 MOORE, PATTY. "Baroque Comedy in Royal Flash." Dallas Morning News (21 October).
Film is "amusing" as opposed to The Three Musketeers, which "delighted." Major flaws are the silliness of the gags and the unloveable Flashman, but the movie is "roguish and usually right." [NB, Card 63.]

492 MUNROE, DALE. "The Four Musketeers." Film Bulletin, 44
      (April/May), 34.
           The film is much the same as its predecessor, slightly
      less slapstick but entertaining.

493 MURF. "The Four Musketeers." Variety, 278 (12 March), 18.
           "Perhaps the film is a triumph of controlled and deliber-
      ate mediocrity," but it looks like "a clumsy carbon of a bad
      satire on the original."

494 _____. "Royal Flash." Variety, 280 (1 October), 24.
           The film is "overproduced, underplayed." It might have
      been better if Lester had pulled out all the stops.

495 NOTH, DOMINIQUE PAUL. Review of Royal Flash. Milwaukee Jour-
      nal TV Screen (9 November), p. 34.
           Film is one of three cited in a commentary on current
      film comedy. It lacks the deeper nuances of the Musketeers
      films; furthermore the actors seem uncertain how straight
      they should be playing.

496 PEARY, GERALD. "We Bombed in Mid-Ocean." Jump-Cut, No. 6
      (March/April), p. 5.
           The conclusion of Juggernaut is "dandy, totally satisfy-
      ing" thanks to the tension created by Fallon's need to out-
      guess Juggernaut. The soap-opera subplots are second to
      Lester's "sharp narrative tale." The film's major mistake
      is the way the women characters are "roped off from the
      action."

497 PETRYNI, MIKE. "Humor in Royal Flash Is Stale and Silly."
      Arizona Republic (26 November).
           Film is "lackluster" echo of Musketeers movies; even the
      cast is uninspired. There are some bright moments, but
      Lester has done the same things before, and better.

498 POWELL, DILYS. "Flash In The Pan." Sunday Times [London]
      (13 July), p. 31.
           Royal Flash fails largely due to erroneous casting, par-
      ticularly of McDowell, a "now" actor, in a blatantly "then"
      part; Bates might have been better. Reed is good but seems
      somehow out of place, as do most of the others.

499 _____. Notice of The Four Musketeers. Sunday Times [London]
      (30 March), p. 35.
           Film seems like a collection of leftovers; the action
      seems "clumsier" than that of The Three, and the mixture of
      farce and violence is "uncomfortable."

1975

500   PRATLEY, GERALD [and RICHARD LESTER]. "Richard Lester: Doing
         the Best He Can." <u>Film</u>, No. 23 (February), pp. 16-18.
              Interview on the occasion of the press screening of <u>Jug-
         gernaut</u> deals primarily with that film, but also discusses
         his feelings about his so-called "canon" of films and his
         style, the success of <u>The Three Musketeers</u>, and future
         plans.

501   RAYNS, TONY. "<u>The Four Musketeers (The Revenge of Milady</u>)."
         [BFI] <u>Monthly Film Bulletin</u>, 42 (April), 80-81.
              Credits, synopsis, review. The film is largely "banal"
         and "perfunctory"; the difference between this and other
         "shoddy" sequels is that "this one casts retrospective doubt
         on the achievement of its predecessor."

502   REYHER, LOREN. "<u>Four Musketeers</u> Flops." <u>Wichita Eagle</u> (6
         April).
              The film lacks the force, humor and pace of <u>The Three</u>.
         [<u>NB</u>, Card 17.]

503   RICHARDS, JEFFREY. "<u>The Four Musketeers (The Revenge of Mi-
         lady</u>)." <u>Focus on Film</u>, No. 21 (Summer), p. 12.
              Credits, review. In deciding to dramatize the second
         half of the Dumas novel, "Lester has given himself a problem
         of mood and approach which he has proved unable to surmount."

504   RIPP, JUDITH. "<u>The Four Musketeers</u>." <u>Parents' Magazine</u>, 50
         (May), 10.
              The narrative flow is smoother in this film than in the
         first one. Lester "seems more interested in telling a good
         story than in being clever."

505   ROBINS, CYNTHIA. "<u>Royal Flash</u> Royal Farce." <u>Columbus Evening
         Dispatch</u> [Ohio] (3 November).
              Film has great potential in terms of actors, director,
         and plot, but falls flat, partly due to Lester's "scatter-
         shot" style and lack of transitions. [<u>NB</u>, Card 77.]

506   _____. "Second Version Is Even Better." <u>Columbus Evening Dis-
         patch</u> [Ohio] (25 March).
              As "an organic whole," the <u>Musketeers</u> duology is Lester
         at his best. [<u>NB</u>, Card 17.]

507   ROBINSON, DAVID. "Not Flashy Enough." <u>The Times</u> [London]
         (11 July), p. 8.
              <u>Royal Flash</u> fails because the Fraser books on which it
         is based are themselves take-offs on Anthony Hope and Dumas;
         the jokes are literary. The transposition of Flashman from

"sharp and subjective commentator" on events (in the books) to a passive participant (in the film) harms him. Lester's comic style seems less confident than before.

508 _____. Review of The Four Musketeers. The Times [London] (27 March), p. 15.
Compared to its predecessor, this film seems "haphazardly strung together"; the writing is "clumsy" and the funniest characters have little to do.

509 ROBINSON, KENNETH. "Gambles, Gambols." Spectator, 234 (12 April), 451.
The Four Musketeers, an "ingenuous, fast-moving, and immensely good to look at" film "in the best Lester tradition," makes "impudent entertainment out of something that could have been horribly portentous."

510 _____. "The Least of Lester." Spectator, 235 (19 July), 90.
The "comic sadism" of Royal Flash is unlikeable; it is a pale imitation of the usual Lester serving of "marvelous visual jokes." The good moments presage "better things to come" for Lester fans.

511 ROSENBAUM, DAVID. "Lacklester." Boston Phoenix, 4 (18 November), Section 2, pp. 4, 6.
Royal Flash is badly conceived, acted and directed.

512 ROTTENBERG, DAN. "A Plague of Sequels." Chicago, 24 (July), 74, 76-77.
The Four Musketeers is one of many sequels discussed, and, for the most part, deemed unnecessary. It is seen as a dishing-up of leftovers, a "new low in brazenness" for Lester.

513 RUSSELL, CANDICE. "Royal Flash Rousing, Satirical Swashbuckler." Miami Herald (18 November).
The film is better than the similar Musketeers movies because "its loving satire isn't overblown." [NB, Card 77.]

514 SARRIS, ANDREW. Notice of The Four Musketeers. Village Voice, 20 (31 March), 70.
Film is superior to The Three because it completes and resolves the story--"the twilight is more beautiful than the dawn."

515 SCHICKEL, RICHARD. "Historical Farce." Time, 105 (7 April), 72-73.

1975

> In The Four Musketeers, Lester is satirizing not only the
> overblown historical epic but history itself, especially the
> zealots who allow themselves to be led by fools and vil-
> lains. Lester is "more than a nimble comic stylist" because
> he has "moral indignation, and the wit to show it only in
> bright, bitter, almost subliminal flashes."

516 SCHIER, ERNEST. "4 Musketeers Swashbuckle Across Area Screens."
Evening Bulletin [Philadelphia] (27 March).
Film is "romantic, melodramatic, equally as handsome as
the first half"; dramatically it is "as good or better,"
with some interestingly staged duels and gags. [NB, Card
17.]

517 SHALIT, GENE. "Time for Larks." Ladies' Home Journal, 92
(June), 8, 15.
Notice of The Four Musketeers calls it "just plain fun"
for children and adults alike.

518 SHERE, CHARLES. "The Last Gags of the Musketeers." Oakland
Tribune (25 March).
The two Musketeers films complement one another while
also standing alone. The Four Musketeers has a bit more
substance, with an ending that is noticeably bitter and
cynical. [NB, Card 17.]

519 SHOREY, KENNETH PAUL. "Four Musketeers Icing on a Delicious
Cake." Birmingham News [Alabama] (13 March).
Film is as enjoyable as its predecessor; reprint of the
author's comments on that film. [NB, Card 17.]

520 SIMON, JOHN. Review of Royal Flash. New York, 8 (13 October),
88.
Lester hit his peak with A Hard Day's Night and has been
declining ever since. It is doubtful that anyone could have
gotten an amusing film from the Royal Flash novel; this production is boring from direction to acting to photography.

521 SINEUX, MICHEL. "Juggernaut (Terreur Sur le Pacific)." Positif, No. 166.
[Cited in Eyquem, no. 446.]

522 SISKEL, GENE. "Richard Lester's Royal Flash." Chicago
Tribune (14 October), Section 3, p. 5.
The missing ingredient is interest or sympathy for any
of the characters. Lester needs to come up with an entirely new approach.

523 ____. "A Sequel to the Musketeers." Chicago Tribune (31
March), Section 3, p. 15.
The Four Musketeers is more enjoyable, more true to the
novel than its predecessor.

524 SLOCUM, BETH. "Four Musketeers Is More of Same." Milwaukee
Journal Accent (23 March), p. 2.
Like the first film, this one contains "more than enough"
bumbling slapstick; there is little character development,
and the battle scenes merely provide more opportunities for
slapstick.

525 SMITH, DOUG. "Musketeers (Part 2) a Delightful Followup."
Omaha World Herald (26 March).
In The Four Musketeers, Lester sends up the material, but
ultimately respects it enough to "get it right," particularly the action sequences and the final duel. [NB, Card 17.]

526 ____. "Royal Flash Falls on Short Side of Hilarity." Omaha
World Herald (21 November).
Although the film is in the same vein as the Musketeers
films--comedy interlaced with glimpses of squalor--it lacks
"former inspiration." [NB, Card 77.]

527 SMITH, LIZ. "Flashy." Cosmopolitan, 179 (December), 20.
Royal Flash is filled with "authentic trivia"; the action is "wonderfully ridiculous," the scenery beautiful.

528 SOPHEIA, DALE. Review of The Four Musketeers. Primo Times
[Bloomington, Indiana], No. 16 (26 May), p. 5.

529 STABINER, KAREN. "Needless Violence Mars Sequel." Santa
Barbara News and Review, 4 (21 March), 21.
The Four Musketeers doesn't work as well as Godfather
Part 2 because it must continue the same story rather than
springboard from the original. The result is "an often
clumsy combination of romanticism and gratuitous violence."
The realness of the blood and death suggest that a deeper
film, complementary to the lunacy of the first swashbuckler,
could have been made. As it is, The Four Musketeers is a
superficial action film.

530 ____. "A Royal Flash That Doesn't Pan Out." Santa Barbara
News and Review, 4 (5 December), 31.
Film is a "sloppy mutation" of Lester's earlier films.
The broad humor blunts its pretensions to satire, and it
isn't funny enough for farce; the treatment of all the wo-
men as "sex-starved little tigresses" is sexist. The

1975

"acerbic, flip perceptiveness" of Lester's earlier work is
sorely missed.

531 STARK, SUSAN. "The Scenery Is Nice But This Tale of Derring-Do
Is Too Sloppily Done." Detroit Free Press (29 October).
Royal Flash is an "exceedingly tiresome effort" due to
its morass of plot and predictability of humor. [NB, Card
63.]

532 STERRITT, DAVID. "Bungling Your Way to Military Glory."
Christian Science Monitor [Eastern edition], 67 (7 Novem-
ber), 18.
Review of Royal Flash.

533 _____. "Egad! It's Those Musketeers Again." Christian Science Monitor [Eastern edition], 67 (30 April), 16.
The Four Musketeers is somewhat disappointing; it should
have been funnier, or else, like Dumas, darker and more
passionate.

534 TESSIER, MAX. "Royal Flash." Écran, No. 42 (15 November),
p. 71.
Lester's earlier epic-parodies were disasters, as is
this film, despite the fine cast and beautiful production.
In French.

535 THOMAS, BARBARA. "Lester's Royal Flash An Indecent Exposure."
Atlanta Journal (30 October).
Film is only occasionally amusing, the direction is
"stale," and the actors uncharacteristically dull. [NB,
Card 63.]

536 VINCENT, MAL. "Four Musketeers a Beguiling Sequel." Virginian-Pilot [Norfolk] (28 March).
The film is not as much of a romp as the first, "more
concerned with plot development." It is equally rich in
period detail and is handsome to look at. [NB, Card 17.]

537 _____. "Royal Flash a Beggar." Virginian-Pilot [Norfolk]
(29 November).
The film is inferior to its predecessors; it is neither
adventure nor parody, and there is an excess of plot. [NB,
Card 77.]

538 WESTERBECK, COLIN L., JR. "Flashback." Commonweal, 102 (5 December), 590, 595.
Compares Royal Flash with another film similar in setting
but not in tone, Conduct Unbecoming. Both expose the

"beast" lurking under the civilized veneer, but Conduct involves while Royal Flash detaches. The lush photography works against the latter's comedy; in the Musketeers films, there were four heroes to offset this effect. Here there is only one, and he can't manage it.

539 WHITMAN, MARK. "Royal Flash." Films Illustrated, 4 (August), 444.
     The film hasn't as much zest and style as the Musketeers movies, but it is a fun action adventure. Includes a note on Alan Bates.

540 WILLIAMS, JOHN [and MALCOLM McDOWELL]. "Entertaining Mr. Flashman." Films Illustrated, 4 (August), 460-61.
     Interview touches briefly on Royal Flash.

541 WINE, BILL. "Four Musketeers--Three's Company, Four's a Crowd." Drummer [Philadelphia], No. 344 (15 April), p. 14.
     If the film were shown as the second half of an epic, as originally planned, it would work better; shown separately, its timing and pace are off.

542 YACOWAR, MAURICE. "Recent Popular Genre Movies: Awash and Aware." Journal of Popular Film, 4 (No. 4) 297-305.
     The ship in Juggernaut is seen as the British Ship of State, and the problems of it and its passengers are allegories for Britain's problems socially, politically, economically, etc.

543 ZIMMERMAN, PAUL D. "None for All." Newsweek, 85 (7 April), 83.
     As the "fun and games" of the first film become deadly in The Four Musketeers, the villains dominate the story. The film is "icy and artfully executed without the pretense to light-heartedness that falsified its predecessor."

1976

544 ALLEN, TOM, S.C. "Down the Years with Robin Hood." America, 134 (20 March), 236-37.
     Lester has always been a furtive romantic; the reason that Robin and Marian and most of his other films succeed where Royal Flash fails is that under the latter's mock derision lies only more mock derision. The others have romanticism and affection under their satiric surfaces.

1976

545 AMES, KATRINE. "Cockeyed Robin." Newsweek, 87 (22 March),
       83-84.
           Although Robin and Marian may be well-intentioned, it
       wastes its cast, due to the director's and writer's lack of
       a "sense of purpose."

546 AMRHINE, KAREN. "Movie Begins Where Legend Ends." News and
       Courier [Charleston, South Carolina] (1 May).
           Lester and the cast of Robin and Marian "enhance rather
       than mar myth" despite the "far-fetched" concept of humaniz-
       ing legends. [NB, Card 41.]

547 ANDREWS, RENA. "You'll Love Robin and Marian." Denver Post
       (16 April).
           The film is "flawed" but its "unabashed" sentimentality
       is refreshing. Lester's comments on "lost ideals, the elu-
       siveness of time and the sadness for what never will be re-
       captured" are poignant and well-done, despite the script's
       duality of approach. [NB, Card 26.]

548 ANON. "Age Comes to Sherwood and an Older but Wiser Robin."
       Minneapolis Tribune (6 April).
           Goldman's script is "one of several splendors" in Robin
       and Marian. This film is mellower than the Musketeers
       films in its depiction of the squalor of history: there is
       room for a little true nobility and romanticism. [NB, Card
       26.]

549 ANON. "Audrey's Back; Robin's Got Her." Waterbury Republican
       [Connecticut] (16 May).
           Robin and Marian's message, about the futility of war,
       is a modern one. The romance succeeds due to the pairing
       of Connery and Hepburn. [NB, Card 41.]

550 ANON. "Briars in Forest Slow Geritol Set." Virginian-Pilot
       [Norfolk] (7 May).
           Review of Robin and Marian. [NB, Card 55.]

551 ANON. "Richard Lester's Robin and Marian." Films and Filming,
       22 (April), 25-28.
           Photo preview.

552 ANON. "The Ritz." Creative Loafing [Atlanta], 5 (6 November),
       13.
           Film is funny "for people of all sexual persuasions,"
       though clean enough for TV.

1976

553 ANON. "Ritz Crackers." Films Illustrated, 6 (November), 108-
111.
Production photos and stills from film.

554 ANON. "Robin and Marion [sic]." El Paso Times (16 May).
Film is an "enchanting fairy tale for adults," bearing
Lester's particular style of humor. The script is unevenly
balanced between humor and drama. [NB, Card 41.]

555 ANON. "Robin Hood Is Returned, This Time with Realism." News
and Observer [Raleigh, North Carolina] (22 April).
Robin and Marian is "novel," Lester's direction is rela-
tively restrained, bringing "a surprising degree of humanity
to the epic form." The acting is "splendid." [NB, Card
26.]

556 ANON. "Robin Returns, with Joy and Sadness." Plain Dealer
[Cleveland] (1 April).
Robin and Marian's dialog is "scintillating," the film
"fascinating." The performances are fine. [NB, Card 26.]

557 ANON. "Rocking-Chair Robin." Courier-Journal [Louisville,
Kentucky] (9 May).
Robin and Marian is appealing because of its uncommon
pro-age bias. Discusses the middle-age career resurgences
of Connery, Lester and Hepburn. [NB, Card 41.]

558 ANON. "Would You Ever Believe an Elderly Robin Hood?" Evening
Bulletin [Philadelphia] (21 March).
Discusses the Robin Hood legends, and the film versions
of them, and facetiously challenges the right of Lester and
Robin and Marian to debunk them. [NB, Card 26.]

559 ANSEN, DAVID. "Robin & Carole & Clark & Marian." Real Paper
[Boston], 5 (7 April), 28.
In Robin and Marian, Lester, whose style has been mellow-
ing, is able to play the story straight when it is necessary. Goldman's ambiguity about his characters nearly
scuttles the story, but the actors--the extraordinary Connery and Hepburn, the fascinating Williamson, Shaw and Harris, and the thoroughly professional supporting actors--
keep it afloat.

560 ARNOLD, GARY. "Robin and Marian, Connery and Hepburn." Washington Post (31 March), Section F, pp. 1, 11.
The film is a "keen disappointment" due to Goldman's
"heartless" script which continually undermines the Connery-
Hepburn rapport. The screenplay makes Robin's motivations
unconvincing and betrays Hepburn's unique qualities.

1976

561 ARNOLD, JAMES. "Robin and Marian and Cupid." Milwaukee Journal Insight (23 May), p. 39.
      Lester and Goldman are to be commended for daring to do
a non-ironic romantic movie with full-out speeches. Lester
is probably "a closet Douglas Fairbanks freak"; for all the
jokes, his action sequences are the best since the Golden
Era. Goldman is probably right that the characters are a
little mad, in love with danger and the "impossible ges-
ture"--if they were sensible, they wouldn't be legends.

562 BATCHELOR, RUTH. "Destroying the Robin Hood Fantasy." Los
Angeles Free Press, 13 (2 April), 13.
      Robin and Marian is unsatisfying because legends aren't
meant to be destroyed. The cast, particularly the leads,
are endearing.

563 BEALE, LEWIS. "Gays and Dolls: the Hollywood Swisheroo."
Drummer [Philadelphia], No. 422 (5 October), p. 22.
      The Ritz is very funny in spite of Lester's "pedestrian"
direction and faults of pace. The screenplay and the actors
carry the film.

564 BILLINGTON, MICHAEL. "Artistic Schizophrenia." Illustrated
London News, 264 (July), 59.
      Robin and Marian doesn't know if it wants to perpetuate
or debunk myths. The actors are good to watch, but "romance and farce make strange bedfellows."

565 BROWN, GEOFF. "Robin and Marian." [BFI] Monthly Film Bulletin, 43 (May), 105.
      Credits, synopsis, review which finds Lester's comic
sense weakening. The script is troubled with "sagging
dramatic tension" and "fuzzy characterizations."

566 CALUM, PER. "Royal Flash--Flashman, den Uovervindelige."
Kosmorama, 22 (Spring), 89.
      Review, in Danish.

567 CANBY, VINCENT. "Robin Hood Gets Older at Music Hall." New
York Times (12 March), p. 26.
      The "curious and contradictory" Robin and Marian works
best as a love story. It is surprising that the "grand
opera" finale works at all, but in doing so it makes some
of the previous clowning "almost intolerable."

568 _____. "Robin's Back and Marian's Got Him." New York Times
(14 March), Section 2, pp. 1, 13.
      Development of No. 567.

569   CARROLL, KATHLEEN. "Fallen Archers." <u>New York Daily News</u>
       (12 March).
            <u>Robin and Marian</u> delivers less than it offers. The Gold-
       man script is ponderous, and Lester is <u>too</u> restrained in his
       direction. [<u>NB</u>, Card 26.]

570   _____. "<u>The Ritz</u> Is the Pits in Drag." <u>New York Daily News</u>
       (13 August).
            Review. [<u>NB</u>, Card 55.]

571   COCKS, JAY. "Bubble Bath." <u>Time</u>, 108 (30 August), 72-73.
            <u>The Ritz</u> is "antic, frantic, mechanical but amusing,"
       with a funny cast. It is the first major film about homo-
       sexuals with no pretensions to "redeeming social value."

572   _____. "Champions." <u>Time</u>, 107 (22 March), 78-79.
            <u>Robin and Marian</u> is "sentimental, flawed and quite won-
       derful," due to its script, director and stars. Followed
       by an article on Hepburn.

573   COLEMAN, JOHN. "Derring-Done." <u>New Statesman</u>, 91 (28 May),
       724.
            The treatment of the romance in <u>Robin and Marian</u> is a
       "tour de force, managed with magnificent dignity and convic-
       tion by actors and director alike." The symbolic rotten
       apples at the beginning and end of the film are objection-
       able.

574   CORLISS, RICHARD. "Funny Peculiar." <u>New Times</u>, 7 (20 August),
       62-63.
            Discussion of the nature of comedy in relation to several
       current comedies. <u>The Ritz</u> suffers from its faithfulness to
       the play and possibly from its director. Billy Wilder is
       suggested as an alternative.

575   _____. "Robbin' and Marryin'." <u>New Times</u>, 6 (2 April), 62,
       64.
            · First hour of <u>Robin and Marian</u> is split between romance,
       war, and squalor. Finally, the romance takes over despite
       Lester's tendency to turn his historical films into "penny
       postcard Hogarth." The characteristic Lesterian touches
       don't mix well with the love story and are thankfully aban-
       doned toward the middle. This is an actors' movie, and
       Connery and Hepburn are superb.

576   CRIST, JUDITH. "Keeping It All in the Family." <u>Saturday Re-
       view</u>, 3 (4 September), 54-55.

1976

> The Ritz is smart but farcical, skilfully made cinematic
> by McNally, and directed by Lester with the breeziness that
> characterized his earlier films.

577 CRIST, JUDITH. "Sherwood Ever After." Saturday Review, 3
     (17 April), 44.
     Present times require neither cynical nor nostalgic looks
at history. Robin and Marian hits just the right blend of
the two, being "sardonic but temperate." Goldman and Lester
both understand the realism underlying romanticism, the
human frailty of heroes.

578 CUFF, HASLETT. "The State of the Art: A Surfeit of 'Fag'
     Jokes." Georgia Straight [Vancouver, Canada], 10 (7 Octo-
ber), 18-19.
     The film of The Ritz is "the most outrageously funny that
Dick Lester has ever lent his rashly brilliant hand to."
The situations and dialog are hokey, silly and hilarious;
Moreno is "enchanting."

579 _____. "Swan Song of a Mythic Figure." Georgia Straight [Van-
couver, Canada], 10 (8 April), 16.
     In Robin and Marian Lester has "again achieved filmic
excellence." The film is sad, funny, charming; the scenes
between Robin and Marian are tender and "heart-wrenching"
but never "sloppy."

580 DENBY, DAVID. "Out of the Closet, Into the Titters." Boston
     Phoenix, 5 (12 October), Section 2, pp. 2, 21.
     The Ritz is very badly directed; few of the actors are
allowed to utilize their talents.

581 DIETRICH, JEAN. "Results Mixed in Romantic Robin, Marian."
     Louisville Defender [Kentucky] (1 April).
     Stars are responsible for the most moving moments in a
"love story as touching as some of the best from an earlier
Hollywood." The Goldman script and Lester's restrained direction are praiseworthy. [NB, Card 26.]

582 EBERT, ROGER. Review of A Hard Day's Night. Chicago Sun-
     Times TV Preview (18 July), p. 4.
     The film is "alive and vibrating and irreverent and fun-
ny"; Lester alternates "manic energy with quiet insights."
It is "one of the 1960's movies that will survive."

583 _____. "Robin and Marian, Love and Death." Chicago Sun-Times
     (21 April).

Film is "partly successful." Lester and Goldman are uncertain how they want to play it, but the film is redeemed
by Connery's and Hepburn's performances. [NB, Card 26.]

584   EDER, RICHARD. "Screen: An Unfunny Thing Happened to The
Ritz." New York Times (13 August), Section C, p. 12.
The film is tolerably funny, but suffers from a lack of
spontaneity and from a surfeit of "male homosexual stomachs,
arms and faces at too short a range."

585   F., T. "Robin, Marian Is Nostalgia Kick." Commercial Appeal
[Memphis] (17 April).
Film is "inconsistent" in its "uneasy" blend of comedy
and drama, but it ultimately comes together. [NB, Card 26.]

586   FORSHEY, GERALD. "Middle-Aged Myths." Christian Century, 93
(23 June), 600.
As the 1930's version of the Robin Hood story was suitable to that time, so is Robin and Marian suited to the disillusioned 70's. Lester successfully mixes farce and sub-
tlety, classicism and romanticism, as he tears down the
myths around Robin, Richard Lionheart, etc. At the same
time he points out that as one ages, one's "necessary myths"
are "less likely to be death-defying than life-sustaining."

587   FRENCH, PHILIP. "Middle Age in the Middle Ages." The Times
[London] (28 May), p. 11.
Robin and Marian is sensitively filmed, the humor much
less forced and the milieu more natural and less commented-
on than in the usual Lester fare. Ultimately, there is
"strain" because it is neither all-involving nor all-detach-
ing.

588   GARDNER, R. H. "Robin and Marian a Waste of Talent." Sun
[Baltimore] (19 April).
Film is "the greatest waste of talent" since The Four
Musketeers. The approaches of Lester and Goldman are con-
fusing and inconsistent. [NB, Card 26.]

589   GERBER, ERIC. "Robin and Marian." Houston Post (2 April).
There is a conflict between Goldman's "earnestness" and
Lester's flippancy. Given the premise that "legend" can be
burdensome to the legendary who can no longer live up to
it, Marian's "euthanasia" is logical but still not "comfortable." [NB, Card 26.]

590   GILLIATT, PENELOPE. "Toujours Gai." New Yorker, 52 (23 August), 70-71.

1976

>   Film of <u>The Ritz</u> lacks the poignancy of the play, pos-
> sibly because it is a heterosexual's treatment of homo-
> sexuals or because it is episodic. It is "splendiferously
> funny" as well as "mysteriously companionable" like many of
> Lester's other films.

591   GOHRING, GARY. "Lack of Depth Hurts <u>The Front</u> and <u>The Ritz</u>."
>   <u>New Times</u> [Tempe, Arizona], 8 (10 November), A7.
>   <u>The Ritz</u> has no meaning beyond its entertainment value,
> which is sufficient if one's expectations are kept low.

592   GOLDMAN, JAMES. <u>Robin and Marian</u>. New York: Bantam Books,
>   Inc., 186 pp.
>   Screenplay (non-spoken parts are written as prose narra-
> tive). In introductory chapters Goldman outlines his rea-
> sons for and approach to writing about Robin Hood, and de-
> scribes the processes involved in getting the screenplay
> bought and filmed.

593   GOW, GORDON. "<u>Robin and Marian</u>." <u>Films and Filming</u>, 22
>   (June), 28-29.
>   Lester keeps a surprisingly straight face. Although one
> wouldn't always wish to see such grim realism, it is well-
> done.

594   HARDY, PETER. "<u>Robin and Marian</u>." <u>Carolina</u>, 1 (8 April), 6.
>   Direction, cast and photography are all outstanding, but
> Goldman can't decide what he's trying to say about heroism.

595   HARTL, JOHN. "Stars Shine in <u>Robin, Marian</u>." <u>Seattle Times</u>
>   (2 April).
>   Film is "not all it could or should have been" due to
> unenergetic writing which has been given an insufficient
> boost by Lester's direction. The whole cast suffers from
> the script's "cuteness" although there are good performances
> and some good scenes. [<u>NB</u>, Card 26.]

596   INMAN, RICK. "<u>Robin and Marian</u>." <u>Bugle American</u> [Milwaukee],
>   7 (30 April), 32-33.
>   Review.

597   JANES, JEREMY. "Leaping Thru Middle Age in Sherwood Forest."
>   <u>Santa Barbara News and Review</u>, 5 (12 May), 24.
>   Lester is a past master at deflating myth; in <u>Robin and</u>
> <u>Marian</u> Richard Lionheart suffers most. The film does very
> well when focusing on "the fallibility of heroes" and the
> "bloody absurdities of battle," but loses its grip on the
> rekindled love affair; it is disastrously "cute" and

ultimately predictable. Lester doesn't quite know how to direct Hepburn, and his polite deference undermines her part as well as the total film.

598   _____. "Risque _Ritz_ Rich in Comedy." _Santa Barbara News and Review_, 5 (12 November), 25.
       Film shows the durability of the classic farce form. Although this is Lester's least personal film in years, his control never wavers. The actors perform well, sometimes brilliantly.

599   JOHNSON, CHARLES. "Should You Laugh, Cry or Cringe?" _Sacramento Bee_ (3 April).
       Robin and Marian has "something for everyone" but ultimately not enough for anybody. It holds together well enough while one is watching it, but afterwards it seems "diffuse." [_NB_, Card 26.]

600   JOHNSON, MALCOLM L. "Lester's _Robin and Marian_." _Hartford Courant_ [Connecticut] (25 April).
       Film resembles the _Musketeers_ films in that Lester "tries to show the larger society as the victims of the antihero's thoughtless exploits." [_NB_, Card 26.]

601   KAEL, PAULINE. "Suicide Is Painless." _New Yorker_, 52 (22 March), 111-13.
       Olivier once said that an actor is unable to play heroes while young because he wants to debunk them. This is true of Connery, who can now "let out the stops." The script of _Robin and Marian_ betrays him and Hepburn, not allowing "the emotion in them to break through into the story." Lester seems more in tune with the actors, who represent "plain glorious feeling," than with the script's "grandeur of sentiment." The rhetoric is anti-Lesterian, and the sidelines mutterers who give "gibbering vitality" to his films are absent. The denouement is disgusting.

602   KAUFFMANN, STANLEY. "_The Ritz_." _New Republic_, 175 (11 September), 25.
       Film is similar to _A Funny Thing Happened on the Way to the Forum_ in its uneasy cinematic style. Part of its problem may be its faithfulness to the play, which is kept intact, unlike _The Knack_, which Lester exploded and reassembled in "a new and brilliant cinematic shape."

603   _____. "Script Troubles." _New Republic_, 174 (27 March), 22.
       The script of _Robin and Marian_ is weak. Hepburn does "well," Connery does not; the rest of the cast is "superb."

1976

Lester, using a different approach than usual, gets some
nice visual effects. The film is "exceptionally well-made
flapdoodle"--not to be confused with good flapdoodle.

604   KING, MIKE. "Pits & Bits & Tits--Ritz." New Haven Advocate
      [Connecticut], 2 (24 November), 22.
          As usual, the thin plot is a framework on which to hang
      Lesterian comedy. Moreno adds a lightness to the film "that
      its careful treatment of the 'gay subculture' prevents."
      The film can't be expected to win any converts to homosexu-
      ality, but it may help by making it less sinister. Re-
      printed in Hartford Advocate, 2 (1 December), 22.

605   KOPKIND, ANDREW. "Limp Ritz." Real Paper [Boston], 5 (23 Oc-
      tober), 46-47.
          The film is less offensive to gays than to Italians, wo-
      men, garbage collectors, etc. However, the "one-situation"
      movie fails because of faulty pace and a lack of tightness.

606   KROLL, JACK. "Tawdry Towels." Newsweek, 88 (30 August), 74.
          Film of The Ritz fails where the play was partly suc-
      cessful because the closeness of the film destroys the ef-
      fective "rabbit warren" look of the multi-leveled set and
      turns stylishness to vulgarity.

607   LAUBACH, DAVID. "A Festival of Unfunny Fag Jokes." Valley
      Advocate [Amherst, Massachusetts], 4 (10 November), 22.
          Another evidence of Lester's artistic decline, The Ritz
      is allowed to trundle along without help from Lester or his
      cameraman. The jokes at the expense of gays are objection-
      able.

608   LAURSEN, BYRON. Review of Robin and Marian. Willamette Valley
      Observer [Eugene, Oregon], 1 (16 April), 6b.
          Lester begins by trying to be clever, but stops before
      he becomes "obnoxious." The film is a "triumph" for its
      lead actors; although "sentimental, escapist and romantic,"
      it has just enough "directorial irony" to make it good to
      watch.

609   LUNDEGAARD, BOB. "At the Movies." Minneapolis Tribune (25
      April).
          In Robin and Marian, Lester is romantic about the lovers,
      but anti-romantic when depicting an old warrior creaking
      into battle. The film is clearly his, but his moods make
      it less satisfying then it could be. [NB, Card 26.]

610 McELFRESH, TOM. "The Romantic Hero Returns for Last Reel."
Cincinnati Enquirer (3 April).
Robin and Marian is like a grownup sequel to Huckleberry
Finn; times and characters have changed, not always for the
better. Lester's style is "hard-edge lyricism"; his theme
is, simply, "the decline of the hero." [NB, Card 26.]

611 McGILLIGAN, PAT. "Legend and Near-Legend: Robin Hood and
Audrey Hepburn." Boston Globe (21 March).
Robin and Marian is "disappointing and uneven." Most of
the article is devoted to coverage of the film's New York
premiere gala and an interview with Hepburn. [NB, Card 26.]

612 MACKLIN, F. ANTHONY. "Robin and Marian." Film Heritage, 11
(Summer), 42-43.
Goldman and Lester have created a "graphic vision of mor-
tality" in which violence mixes with "tenderness and ironic
humanity."

613 MAHAR, TED. "Erroll Flynn, You've Grayed." Oregonian [Port-
land] (8 April).
Robin and Marian is "intelligent, sensitive, gorgeously
photographed"; the humor is, for Lester, subdued, but traces
of his "iconoclastic wit" still remain. Hepburn's presence
is a treat for audiences. [NB, Card 26.]

614 MATSON, BRIAN. "The Ritz." Iconoclast [Dallas], 10 (22 October), 15, 16.
The film medium allows expansion and clarification of
the story line. The lack of deep "meaning" does not lessen
the fun.

615 MICHAEL, FRED. "Acting Makes Sherwood Forest Heroics Succeed."
North Carolina Anvil, 10 (10 April), 9.
Robin and Marian's "magic" is that of Audrey Hepburn.
The script is "terrible" and fails to move us as it should.
The lead actors are solely responsible for its working at
all.

616 _____. "Farce Showcases Flamboyant Rita Moreno." North Carolina Anvil, 10 (4 November), 8.
The Ritz works despite Lester, who does little to keep
it going. Moreno is the prime element in its success.

617 MILLER, JEANNE. "Poor Stealing from Rich Tale." San Francisco
Examiner (1 April).
Robin and Marian is "dismal and violent"; Lester seems
not to know whether he wants to debunk myths or make

1976

romantic drama--he fails at both. The film lacks original-
ity and dramatic tension. [NB, Card 26.]

618   MILLS, DONIA. "Robin and Marian Grow Old Ungracefully."
       Washington Star (1 April).
            The film is a "sour little trifle"; the screenwriter is
       "arch and highhanded." Lester has done too many anti-heroic
       films, so that this one looks prefabricated. "Lester's mis-
       chievous streak is forever crossing swords with Goldman's
       pomposity." [NB, Card 26.]

619   MURF. "The Ritz." Variety, 284 (11 August), 19.
            Review.

620   _____. "Robin and Marian." Variety, 282 (10 March), 22.
            The film is "disappointing and embarrassing" because it
       is awkward in its duality and doesn't fulfill the potential
       of its artists. The stars aren't as young as they used to
       be, and their attempts at dash are "pitiable."

621   NOTH, DOMINIQUE PAUL. "Robin Returns a Bit Jaded." Milwaukee
       Journal (9 April).
            Robin and Marian is "tremendously entertaining" but it
       does too many different things. It is redeemed by Hepburn
       et al. Lester has "bent too easily" to Goldman's lyricism,
       losing his satirical bite. [NB, Card 26.]

622   OREN, ALLEN. "A Legend's Revisited in Robin and Marian."
       Charlotte Observer [North Carolina] (22 April).
            There are errors of logic in the film's plot, and errors
       in filming consistency. Lester's vision is realistic but
       the comedy is too pat, "the dialog unnaturally fine-phrased."
       The acting is "superb." [NB, Card 26.]

623   PERSICO, JOYCE J. "Robin and Marian." Trenton Times [New
       Jersey] (11 April).
            Problems of love and age are handled "tipsily" by Gold-
       man. His stress on age and Lester's on comedy make the
       film an "irresistible and unusual surprise." The romance
       is pure and "marvelous." [NB, Card 26.]

624   PETRYNI, MIKE. "Robin Fails On Target." Arizona Republic
       [Phoenix] (7 April).
            Robin and Marian inexplicably fails to live up to the
       promise given by talented artists. It is "almost" what it
       should have been. [NB, Card 26.]

625   POLMAN, JEFFREY. "Robin and Marian: Cute and Dumb." Hartford
      Advocate [Connecticut], 2 (12 May), 18.
          If the original Robin Hood story didn't exist, "this
      would be a great film." However, Lester takes liberties
      with a story he assumes everyone knows, fails to establish
      "personal traits," and expects the audience to be involved.

626   PYM, JOHN. "The Ritz." [BFI] Monthly Film Bulletin, 43 (De-
      cember), 255-56.
          Credits, synopsis, review which says that the film suc-
      ceeds despite Lester, mostly because the original work is
      so strong. Lester slows down the pace and reduces the mul-
      ti-leveled action of the stage play and changes the view-
      point somewhat so that the audience feels like "faintly
      embarrassed" outsiders.

627   REED, REX. "The Ritz." Vogue, 166 (September), 239.
          The play has been "bludgeoned" by Lester.

628   REILLY, CHARLES E. "Robin and Marian a Ripoff." Drummer
      [Philadelphia], No. 398 (20 April), p. 21.
          The film succeeds until the ending, whose maudlin morbid-
      ity betrays the story and the legend.

629   REILLY, CHARLES PHILLIPS. "Robin and Marian." Films in Re-
      view, 27 (April), 241.
          The film "partially succeeds" with its witty/boring
      script and with Connery's performance.

630   RICH, FRANK. "Audrey, Sean and All Our Yesterdays." New York
      Post (13 March).
          Discusses film in context of the careers of Connery,
      Hepburn and Lester, each representing a facet of a bygone
      era--James Bond, Holly Golightly and the early Beatles--and
      each having a sort of artistic rebirth with Robin and Mari-
      an. Each has been able to reconcile their past performances
      with their present visions--in Lester's case his "high
      spirits" of the early sixties films and his "new sobriety."
      Comedy is present in Robin and Marian but it doesn't subvert
      story and characters. [NB, Card 26.]

631   _____. "A Beautiful Legend Reborn." New York Post (12 March).
          Shorter, less-developed version of No. 630. [NB, Card
      26.]

632   _____. "On the Way to The Ritz, Richard Lester Got Lost."
      New York Post (13 August).
          Review. [NB, Card 55.]

1976

633   ROSENBAUM, DAVID. "Dying Legend." Boston Phoenix, 5 (6 April),
       Section 2, pp. 2, 12.
            Lester and his actors bring off the "irresistible" idea
       behind Robin and Marian. The characters in the film must
       live their legend; they know they can't "play it safe" and
       that is their "tragedy."

634   SARRIS, ANDREW. "Middle Ages Light Up Music Hall." Village
       Voice, 21 (29 March), 117.
            In Robin and Marian, Lester is "at the peak of his some-
       what disenchanted and fragmented neoclassical form as a di-
       rector." He and Goldman have done their work with "bril-
       liance and conviction" but it is hard to imagine the film
       being so good without any one of its cast.

635   _____. "Putting On The Ritz." Village Voice, 21 (23 August),
       117.
            Review.

636   SCHEPELERN, PETER. "Robin Hood og Marian." Kosmorama, 22
       (Winter), 359.
            Review, in Danish.

637   SCHUMACK, SCOTT WILLIAM. "The Bed-Sitting Room." Cinefantas-
       tique, 5 (Spring), 27.
            The "bizarre and beautiful" film's time has come. Les-
       ter, like Kubrick, has realized that "the words describing
       nuclear slaughter have become meaningless. Only in madness
       is truth, and only in laughter is a defense."

638   SHALIT, GENE. "Classic Tinkering." Ladies' Home Journal, 93
       (June), 12.
            The transformation of legends to mortal status is objec-
       tionable in Robin and Marian, a "story that seldom takes
       flight."

639   SHOREY, KENNETH PAUL. "Robin and Marian Witty, Wise, Romantic;
       Recommended Highly." Birmingham News [Alabama] (9 June).
            Lester, like Kubrick, is "a genius...with his own special
       visions," trying to make them salable. This makes the
       film's anti-Hollywood ending doubly courageous. [NB, Card
       41.]

640   SIMON, JEFF. "Artistry of Connery and Hepburn Makes Robin,
       Marian Come Alive." Buffalo Evening News [New York] (15
       April).
            The film works in spite of Goldman, and because of the
       actors. Lester contributes some beautiful shots and a few
       laughs, but keeps a low profile. [NB, Card 26.]

641   SIMON, JOHN. "Flattening The Ritz, Flattering the Duke." New
      York, 9 (30 August), 50.
          The film fails in part because the play is transposed,
      rather than translated, into cinema. The performances re-
      main broad, and the rabbit-warren of doors through which
      the characters constantly dart should be, but are not, re-
      worked to fit the two-dimensionality of the screen.

642   _____. "Robin Hood and His Merry Menopause." New York, 9
      (29 March), 81-82.
          Robin and Marian's main problem is Goldman's script,
      which juggles history. The film contains comic Lesterian
      touches and serious Lesterian touches, either of which are
      acceptable, but not clumsily mixed as in this film. Two
      major assets are the photography of David Watkin, and the
      actors.

643   SISKEL, GENE. "A Merrie Time with Robin Hood." Chicago
      Tribune (19 April), Section 3, p. 10.
          The action sequences in Robin and Marian are "boring"
      compared to those showing the relationship of Robin with
      his men and with Marian.

644   STERRITT, DAVID. "Three Mythical Heroes Star: Results,
      Mixed." Christian Science Monitor [Midwestern edition], 68
      (24 March), 11.
          Although Robin and Marian doesn't quite work, the tragi-
      comedy has a "depth" which other Lester films have lacked.
      The screenplay is "lackluster."

645   STOOP, NORMA McLAIN. Review of The Ritz. After Dark, 9
      (September), 91.
          Film combines Lester's "frantically paced direction,"
      McNally's "knowing and zany" script, and "performances of
      dizzying skill," the best of which is Moreno's.

646   _____. Review of Robin and Marian. After Dark, 9 (May), 82.
          Film is "moribund," directed with a "faltering hand."

647   TAYLOR, ROBERT. "Old in Merrie Olde." Oakland Tribune (2
      April).
          Robin and Marian is unromantic, unadventurous, unwitty,
      redeemed mostly by the two leads. [NB, Card 26.]

648   TEALE, MUNRO. "Musketeer Goons." Films and Filming, 22
      (February), 4.
          Reader's letter comparing Lester's Musketeers with his
      earlier Goons.

1976

649   THOMAS, BARBARA. "Robin, Marian Pretty, But Movie Is Lacking."
      Atlanta Journal (2 April).
            Film's pluses are its performances and its period sense;
      minuses includes Lester's uncertainty of approach and the
      ending. [NB, Card 26.]

650   WHITMAN, MARK. "Robin and Marian." Films Illustrated, 5
      (June), 366.
            The "goonish" mutterings detract from the story. The di-
      rection is "spirited," but is essentially a writer's film.
      Includes short note on Robert Shaw.

651   WUNTCH, PHILIP. "Robin Hood Legend's Lovingly Renovated."
      Dallas Morning News (2 April).
            Robin and Marian's duality of purpose is troublesome;
      Connery and Hepburn make the story succeed. [NB, Card 26.]

                              1977

652   ANON. "Richard Lester's The Ritz." Films and Filming, 23
      (January), 36-37.
            Photo preview.

653   CEBE, GILLES. "La Rose et La Fleche [The Rose and the Arrow]."
      Écran, No. 56 (March), pp. 55-56.
            Review of Robin and Marian, in French. "Far from explod-
      ing the legend, the filmmaker seeks simply...to explain how
      an ultimately ordinary man...becomes a myth in spite of him-
      self." In doing so, "Lester inters...with a supreme ele-
      gance, a civilization and its myths."

654   GOW, GORDON. "The Ritz." Films and Filming, 23 (January), 35,
      38.
            "The going is often stubbornly unfilmic," as the farce
      bogs down.

655   HIRSCH, PETER [and RICHARD LESTER]. "Møde Med Richard Lester."
      Kosmorama, 23 (Spring), 41-42.
            Interview, in Danish.

656   MALMKJAER, POUL. "Det Går Helt Agurk I Saunen Eller Lester og
      Bøsserne." Kosmorama, 23 (Spring), 40.
            Review of The Ritz, in Danish.

657   RENAUD, TRISTAN. "La Rose et La Fleche." Cinéma, No. 22
      (April), pp. 84-86.

1977

Robin and Marian seeks to immerse its characters in the
atmosphere of their time, the everyday hardships and reali-
ties of the Middle Ages. The "sublime" performances of
Connery and Hepburn are a "miracle." In French.

658   RICHARDS, JEFFREY. Swordsmen of the Screen: From Douglas
      Fairbanks to Michael York. London, Henley and Boston:
      Routledge and Kegan Paul, pp. 54-56, 160-61, 209-10.
          Pp. 54-56 deal with the Musketeers films in relation to
      other versions of the story; 160-61 briefly discuss Royal
      Flash as a variation on the Prisoner of Zenda plot; 209-10
      deal with Robin and Marian, the latest of a long line of
      Robin Hood sagas.

659   VIVIANI, CHRISTIAN. "Tristan et Yseult, Roméo et Juliette,
      Robin et Marianne...(La Rose et La Fleche)." Positif, No.
      189 (January), pp. 62-65.
          Long analysis of several aspects of Robin and Marian:
      the screenplay; the characters (who here become one with
      other mythical couples who only find themselves in death);
      its relationship to Lester's other work, particularly his
      historical epic comedies.

Other Film Work and Writings

1955

*660 CURTAINS FOR HARRY (writer, composer)
Produced by Associated Rediffusion. First original musical comedy on British commercial TV.

1956

*661 DOWNBEAT (director)
Produced by Associated Rediffusion. First commercial-TV jazz show.

*662 THE DICK LESTER SHOW (host, with Alun Owen)
Ad-lib comedy and musical half-hour. Lasted one performance.

*663 A SHOW CALLED FRED (director)
Series of TV Goon Shows with Peter Sellers, Spike Milligan, Harry Secombe.

*664 IDIOT'S WEEKLY (director)
Another title for 663.

*665 SON OF FRED (director)
Another title for 663.

1957

*666 MARK SABRE (director)
Private-eye series. Lester directed thirteen of the season's episodes; the other thirteen were directed by Joseph Losey.

1958

*667   AFTER HOURS (director)

*668   THE GOON SHOW (director)

1959

*669   HAVE JAZZ, WILL TRAVEL (director)
        Short film, pilot for a TV series.

1960

*670   SEA WAR (composer, with Reg Owen)
        War series similar to Victory at Sea.

1969

*671   Interview, with Alexander Walker. Thames Television. Shown
        24 September. Discussed his early days in television, his
        early films, etc.

1975

672   Interview, for Camera Three series. WCBS-TV. Shown in two
       parts, on 16 and 23 March. Discussion of his films from
       the beginning to the Musketeers, with numerous film clips.

Commercials

*673   More than 500 commercials, many of them prize-winners, spread
        over his entire film career. Include ads for Esso, Kodak,
        After-Eight Chocolates, Cadbury Chocolate, Grant's Whiskey,
        Gillette "Spoiler" razor blades, Carnation. Most renowned
        are:
        Acrilan "The Cat"--60 unbroken seconds of a Siamese cat
        prowling through a house on Acrilan carpets. 1966.
        L & M "Dream Love Stamp"--a parody of the film Last Year
        at Marienbad. 1969.
        Braniff International 1975--satiric premonition of the
        Concorde SST whose mood is the opposite of what Braniff in-
        tended. 1967.

Radio

1958

*674   ROUND THE BEND.

Writings

1965

675   "In Search of the Right Knack." Films and Filming, 11 (July),
       14. Discusses the changes he made from the Ann Jellicoe
       stage play of The Knack, and tells why certain scenes were
       done certain ways.

1967

676   "Richard Lester and the Art of Comedy." Film [British],
       No. 48 (Spring), pp. 16-21. Excerpts from a taped inter-
       view touching briefly on films up to Forum; other comments
       deal with his style and his preferences in screen comedy.

1969

*677   "What I Learned from Commercials." Action, 4 (January/Febru-
       ary), 32.

Archival Sources

There are no known collections specifically on Lester; however, the following institutions have material on him.

678   MARGARET HERRICK LIBRARY
       Academy of Motion Picture Arts and Sciences
       8949 Wilshire Blvd.
       Beverly Hills, California 90211
       Phone: (213) 278-8990

       Contains biographical files on Lester, as well as production files, which include clippings, reviews, and stills, on all his feature films.

679   NATIONAL FILM ARCHIVE
       81 Dean Street
       London, W1V 6AA
       England
       Phone: 01-437-4355

       Holdings are exhaustive in the area of books on film and television, and of film periodicals and ephemera. Clipping files are kept on film personalities and directors.

680   LIBRARY OF CONGRESS
       10 First Street S.E.
       Washington, D.C. 20540
       Phone: (202) 426-5840

       Has 35 mm reference prints of all Lester's feature films. They may be viewed at the library, free of charge, by appointment.

Film Distributors

681 COLUMBIA PICTURES, 300 S. Colgems Square, Burbank, California, (213) 843-6000; 711 Fifth Avenue, New York, New York, (212) 751-4000.

  It's Trad, Dad (Ring-a-Ding Rhythm)
  The Ritz (Columbia-Warner)
  Robin and Marian
  The Running, Jumping and Standing Still Film

COLUMBIA-WARNER--See Columbia Pictures.

682 FILMS INCORPORATED (16 mm), 733 Green Bay Road, Wilmette, Illinois 60091, (312) 256-6600; Suite No. 423, Oak Cliff Bank Tower, Dallas, Texas, (214) 941-4236; 35-01 Queens Boulevard, Long Island City, New York 11101, (212) 937-1110; 5589 New Peachtree Road, Atlanta, Georgia 30341, (404), 451-7445; 5625 Hollywood Boulevard, Hollywood, California 90028, (213) 466-5481.

  The Three Musketeers

683 SWANK MOTION PICTURES, INC. (16 mm), 393 Front Street, Hempstead, New York 11556, (516) 538-6500; 7926 Jones Branch Drive, McLean, Virginia 22101, (703) 821-1040; 5200 W. Kennedy Boulevard, Tampa, Florida 32609,(813) 870-0500; 1200 Roosevelt Road, Glen Ellyn, Illinois 60137, (312) 629-9004; 4111 Directors' Row, Houston, Texas 77092, (713) 683-8222; 220 Forbes Road, Braintree, Massachusetts 02184, (617) 848-8300.

  Robin and Marion

684 20TH CENTURY-FOX PICTURES, 10201 W. Pico Boulevard, Los Angeles, California, (213) 277-2111; 1345 Avenue of the Americas, New York, New York, (212) 397-8500.

  The Four Musketeers
  Royal Flash
  The Three Musketeers

143

685 UNITED ARTISTS, 1041 N. Formosa, Los Angeles, California, (213) 851-1234; 727 Seventh Avenue, New York, New York 10019, (212) 575-3000.

> The Bed-Sitting Room
> A Funny Thing Happened on the Way to the Forum
> A Hard Day's Night
> Help!
> How I Won the War
> Juggernaut
> The Knack
> The Mouse on the Moon

686 UNITED ARTISTS 16 (16 mm), 729 Seventh Avenue, New York, New York 10019, (212) 575-4715.

> The Bed-Sitting Room
> A Funny Thing Happened on the Way to the Forum
> A Hard Day's Night
> Help!
> How I Won the War
> Juggernaut
> The Knack
> The Mouse on the Moon

687 WARNER BROTHERS, Warner Brothers/7 Arts Films, 4000 Warner Boulevard, Burbank, California 91522, (213) 843-6000; Warner Brothers Distributing Corp., 75 Rockefeller Plaza, New York, New York, (212) 484-8000.

> Petulia

688 CLEM WILLIAMS FILMS (16 mm), 2240 Noblestown Road, Pittsburgh, Pennsylvania 15205, (412) 921-5810; 1277 Spring Street N.W., Atlanta, Georgia 30309, (404) 872-5353; 5424 W. North Avenue, Chicago, Illinois 60639, (312) 637-3322; 2170 Portsmouth, Houston, Texas 77098, (713) 529-3906.

> Petulia

Author Index

Combs, Richard, 308
Corliss, Richard, 149, 165, 207,
    309, 574, 575
Crist, Judith, 208, 243, 310,
    434, 435, 576, 577
Crowther, Bosley, 24, 40, 72,
    73, 150
Cuff, Haslett, 311, 312, 436,
    437, 578, 579
Cuskelly, Richard, 438
Cutler, Bill, 269

D

Dassinger, George, 313
Davis, Russell E., 439
Dawson, Jan, 151, 209
Delain, Michel, 277
Dempsey, Michael, 267
Denby, David, 580
Dent, Alan, 41, 74, 75, 152
Dietrich, Jean, 440, 581
Dorn, Norman K., 308
Drew, Bernard, 441
Durgnat, Raymond, 25, 76

E

Ebert, Roger, 442, 443, 582, 583
Eder, Richard, 584
Eichelbaum, Stanley, 444
Eliscu, Lita, 210
Engvén, Ingvar, 445
Ennis, Paul, 127
Eyles, Allen, 363
Eyquem, Olivier, 446

F

F., T., 585
Fallowell, Duncan, 314
Farren, Jonathan, 447
Feiffer, Jules, 128
Finocchiaro, Ray, 448, 449
Fitzgibbon, Constantine, 42
Flood, Richard, 450
Fontenia, Cesar S., 77
Forshey, Gerald, 586
Frank, Ellen, 315
French, Philip, 78, 587
Frumkes, Roy, 316

G

G., F. H., 153
Gagnard, Frank, 451
Galligan, Richard, 452
Gallo, William, 453, 454
Gardner, R. H., 455, 588
Geldzahler, Henry, 43
Gelmis, Joseph, 259
Gerber, Eric, 589
Gill, Brendan, 79, 129, 154
Gilliatt, Penelope, 211, 317,
    456, 590
Gilman, Richard, 155
Gohring, Gary, 591
Goldman, Frederick, 268
Goldman, James, 592
Goldstein, Ruth M., 457
Gow, Gordon, 156, 318, 319,
    458-60, 593, 654
Grant, Paul, 461
Green, Benny, 320, 462
Greenspun, Roger, 212
Gross, Leonard, 130
Guarino, Ann, 463
Gubern Garriga-Nogués, Román, 244

H

Hagen, Ray, 44
Hall, William, 278
Halliwell, Leslie, 321, 322
Hampe, Barry, 213
Hanson, Curtis Lee, 157
Harcourt, Peter, 80
Hardaway, Francine, 323, 464
Hardwick, Elizabeth, 81
Hardwick, Michael, 465
Hardy, Peter, 594
Haroldson, Thomas, 158, 214
Hartl, John, 595
Hartung, Philip T., 45, 82, 131,
    159, 215
Hatch, Robert, 83, 160, 216,
    245, 324
Hebeker, Klaus, 84
Hine, Al, 85, 325
Hinxman, Margaret, 270
Hirsch, Peter, 655
Hobson, Harold, 86
Hofsess, John, 326, 466, 467

Film Title Index

DATE DUE